LOYAL TO THE END

THE LIFE AND LETTERS OF QING DYNASTY MINISTER WEN SU

雲中燕

FRANCIS WANN

Loyal to the End

By Francis Wann

Trade Paper: 978-988-8904-34-1
Digital: 978-988-8904-33-4

© 2025 Francis Wann

Cover calligraphy "忠" by Ho Yauwei (何幼惠), whose uncle He Guoli (何國禮, 1859 - 1937), was a Jinshi in 1898, the 24th year of Guangxu reign.

BIOGRAPHY & AUTOBIOGRAPHY

EB235

All rights reserved. No part of this book may be reproduced in material form, by any means, whether graphic, electronic, mechanical or other, including photocopying or information storage, in whole or in part. May not be used to prepare other publications without written permission from the publisher except in the case of brief quotations embodied in critical articles or reviews. For information contact info@earnshawbooks.com

Published in Hong Kong by Earnshaw Books Ltd.

> "If we want to write good poetry,
> why not learn to be a good person first?"
> — Wen Su, on poetry

承烈賢姪 雅鑒

長風吟松晚雨細

破手題詩潑墨斜

戊寅清明溫肅

From as far back as I can remember, a huge yellowish couplet hung in our family sitting room, gathering dust. I was for many years oblivious of its significance. It was addressed from Wen Su to his nephew, my father, and it read:

> 長風吟松晚雨細，
> 醉手題詩淡墨斜。

Long breezes, whispering pines, an evening of drizzle,
I compose this poem with an unsteady hand, the pale ink slanting.

It was signed Wen Su,
and dated the Ching Ming
in the *mu-yin year (1938)*.

Portraiture of Wen Su by a court artisan

WESTERN STYLE PORTRAITURE FOR BOOKLET OF RECORDS OFFICE
Responding to *Chun Yu*[1], deputy director, True Records Institute, c1912

The bath on the west is close to the palace.
With much sadness, I return where my brush is.
It's for occasions of gratitude or obituaries.
I'm leaving my country, but my writings will stay here.
I can no longer follow you to the Three Palace Academies [2]
which still stand before thousands of men.
Don't worry if your face looks like mine.
There's always someone who looks like an angel.

實錄館小集用西法寫照次春榆總裁韻 壬子四月

浴殿西頭尺五天
重來戟筆倍淒然
酬恩寗止文章事
去國猶留翰墨緣
無復肩隨三館後
依然山立萬夫前
莫愁子面如吾面
尚有旁人望若仙

Footnotes:
1. Guo Zengxin郭曾炘(1855-1928), alias Chun Yu, Jinshi in the 6th year of Guangxu (1880), deputy director of the True Records Institute during the first year of Xuantong.
2. The Three Palace Academies comprised the Palace Historiographic Academy, the Palace Secretariat Academy, and the Palace Academy for the Advancement of Literature.

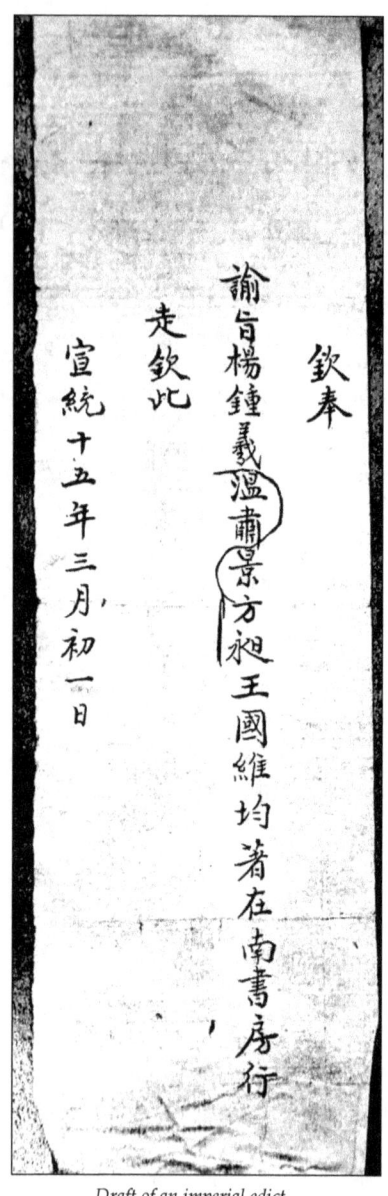

Draft of an imperial edict

FRANCIS WANN

On His Majesty's Service

This decree serves to inform the following
to report for duty at the South Study:

> Yang Zhongxi
> Wen Su
> Jing Fangchang
> Wang Guowei

Dated
this the fifteenth year of Xuantong reign, (1923)
the first day of March

不俗二字豈易言哉

Contents

Steward of the Dragon Throne	3
The Hanlin	9
Who is Wen Su?	17
The History Man	21
The Family Man	35
Friends, Hanlins, & The Connectibles	41
The Letters Man	49
Family Letters	55

Letter #1	57		Letter #15	105
Letter #2	59		Letter #16	109
Letter #3	61		Letter #17	111
Letter #4	63		Letter #18	117
Letter #5	65		Letter #19	121
Letter #6	67		Letter #20	123
Letter #7	71		Letter #21	129
Letter #8	75		Letter #22	131
Letter #9	77		Letter #23	136
Letter #10	81		Letter #24	143
Letter #11	85		Letter #25	145
Letter #12	91		Letter #26	147
Letter #13	95		Letter #27	149
Letter #14	99			

Selected Other Writings — 153

    Lecture On Poetry At The Chinese Society,   153
        University of Hong Kong
    Preface to Lecture Notes on Political Summary
        of Zhenguan (貞觀政要)   157
    Daughter Ah Chiu's Obituary   163
    Letter From Li Zhanzhi   169
    Reply To Li Zhanzhi's Wedding Invite   170
    Poem Dedicated To Chan Dulu On   173
    Zhu Ruzhen's Poem To Wen Su   175
    Recollections From Bifu (Wan Chunghan)   177
    Poem To Wen Su From Zhang Cikang (1923)   179
    … And Afterword To Bifu (1948)   182
    Poem And Postscript By Jin Zhanlin   183
    Letter To Lai Chihsi 1   185
    Letter To Lai Chihsi 2   187
    Message From Bishen   189
    Suffix To Zhu Jiujiang's Examination Script   193

Epilogue — 199
Afterwords — 205
    Dr Wang Liang (王亮)   205
    Professor Cho-Yee To   208
    Dr Esther Woo   210
Acknowledgements — 213
Bibliography — 215

STEWARD OF THE DRAGON THRONE

On February 7, 1906, the intensely anticipated birth of a male infant took place in Beijing. This was no ordinary baby; he was born a Manchu noble and the heir-apparent to the Qing dynasty's Golden Dragon Throne. He was the last emperor of China.

As was the custom, a junior Hanlin Academy scholar, a rising star named Wen Su, was summoned to name the child. He called him Pu Yi, meaning 'proclamation of unity'.

Two years and ten months later, on December 2, 1908, in the Hall of Supreme Harmony within the Forbidden City, Pu Yi was invested as Emperor Xuantong, and Wen Su said in his writings that it was he who placed the two-year-old child on to the throne. As to who exactly had the honor of placing the new emperor on the throne, the accounts differ. Some say that Puyi's father, the prince regent, did it. But *The New York Times*, reporting on the day after the coronation, said Pu Yi "made his way [to the throne] alone and showed no need of assistance that willing hands would have given him had his little feet faltered." It remains a mystery, but it is entirely plausible that the prince regent delegated the duty to this young Hanlin, as Wen Su says.

LOYAL TO THE END

Much is known about the last emperor, but far less is known about the scholar Wen Su who became his tutor and mentor, one who longed for the restoration of an empire that Confucius would have admired, one which in Wen Su's eyes was founded on integrity and honor. He was renowned for his calligraphy. Of his private life, little has previously come to light, however the letters to colleagues and family contained in this volume for the first time open up a new realm of research, in addition to offering many calligraphic gems.

Wen Su was a scholar, a Hanlin, a patriot, a diplomat, a poet, a calligrapher, a father and husband, and a landlord of farmland with mulberry trees and fish ponds. Then there was the inner Wen Su, revealed through his letters.

Scholars of the history of the late Qing will be familiar with the historical context during which the Hanlin officials strove to attain and maintain the highest ideals of governance at a crucial turning point in Chinese history. But for them as well as others, the intimate details of Wen Su's life provides a unique perspective on the fate of an empire.

For essentially all of Wen Su's life, China was beset by internal conflicts, factional infighting, natural disasters, famines, plagues, and pandemics. The Taiping Rebellion, which began in 1850 and lasted for more than a decade, claimed an estimated twenty million casualties. What began with grievances against the Qing government developed into a full-fledged war between the establishment and the people, led by a self-proclaimed prophet Hong Xiuquan. The rebellion was finally suppressed in 1864 by Zeng Guofan (曾國藩), a Hanlin official who managed to restore stability in the Qing Empire, and who became a role model for Wen Su. The end of the rebellion, however, had serious repercussions, namely an accelerated dispersal of power to the provinces and to warlords in the early 20th Century.

The Sino-Japanese War in 1895 left China humiliated with a significant loss of prestige. Korea was removed from its suzerainty, Taiwan and the Liaodong Peninsula were ceded to Japan, and foreign imperial powers forced open more ports for international trade.

China was then battered by the Boxer Uprising (1889-1901), which was anti-foreign, anti-colonial and anti-Christian. For several days in 1900, at the beginning of the siege of the Legation Quarter in Peking, the rebels set fire to buildings next to the British Legation which contained the Hanlin Academy. The Academy was in effect China's national library, and it was severely damaged by the flames. Residents of the legations, including sinologist Edmund Backhouse, tried to save some of the priceless texts stored within these important buildings, but damage was significant and many works were lost.

The Final Protocol to wrap up the Boxer Rebellion, agreed later in 1900 and signed in September the following year, was one of the most devastating and extremely unequal treaties in history, and Chinese people long marked September 7 as a reminder of national shame.

The year 1908 (戊申) had special significance both for Wen Su himself, and for the history of Qing Empire. This year saw the death of the two most senior figures in the Manchu Imperial family. The Emperor Guangxi (1871-1908) died on November 14 and Empress Dowager Cixi, who had been the true ruler of the empire for more than forty years, died one day later on November 15. The deaths were followed by a lengthy period of national mourning with full imperial extravagance, and intensive brokering in the court's corridors of powers.

The political consequence of their deaths was also the coronation of Pu Yi, with his father Zaifeng as Prince Regent.

LOYAL TO THE END

A China suddenly without its de facto ruler the Empress Dowager Cixi certainly marked the end of an era as well as the beginning of a new one. And for the Qing dynasty, established after the Manchu invasion in 1644, it was the beginning of the end. The Qing dynasty collapsed in 1912 and many Hanlin scholars including Wen Su eventually fled to Hong Kong — then a British colony — because of its relative neutrality in terms of Chinese politics. Having worked so closely with the Manchus, these men were under some physical danger in the early days of the Republic. But alarmed at what they saw as a decline in the standards of the Chinese language and culture and the absence of a proper place in Hong Kong for advanced Chinese studies, Wen Su and other Hanlins in 1923 founded the Hok Hoi Library to advance knowledge of Chinese culture. Lectures were held every week, with only a brief interruption during the Japanese occupation in the early 1940s. With more than 30,000 books in its collection, the Library now occupies a special section in the Hong Kong Central Library, under Rare Books. And today, a century after its establishment, the Hok Hoi Library still retains its original tradition of conducting weekly lectures.

Wen Su (Left) with other Hanlins at Guangdong Huizhou Assembly Hall, Beijing (1909)

THE HANLINS

Anyone interested in the history of the late Qing dynasty will be fascinated by the lives of the members of the Hanlin Academy whose existence in the government hierarchy alongside Manchu ministers has often been the subject of intense debate.

The Academy had a long history dating back to the 8th Century. It was created in the Sui dynasty and continued through the Tang, Yuan, Ming and Qing dynasties. It was always regarded as the institution of the highest learning and research with membership strictly confined to an elite group of scholars, carefully selected by invitation only. For intellectuals and academia, for centuries it represented the pinnacle of achievement. These learned men, in the early years of the 20th Century, still led a largely secluded life in the exclusive Academy, but the calls for reform were heard everywhere outside the Forbidden City, and so fierce was the clamor that those inside the walls could no longer pretend their empire would last forever.

By the time of Wen Su, the Academy had been in existence for well over a thousand years, but the Hanlins were definitely an endangered species. The path to the Hanlin Academy was long and winding, and access was still gained through various examinations called keju (科舉), which involved the recommending of new recruits for the civil service in a particular year by local officials. Candidates were mainly tested on the Confucian classics and the teachings of the great sage from 2,500 years before.

The process began with local examinations (鄉試) which were held every three years, and graduates were granted a qualification called Juren (舉人) which made them eligible for the more advanced provincial-level examinations (會試) held in the provincial capitals and usually spread over a week. The best graduates would then be invited to take part in the imperial or palace examinations (殿試), which were also held every three years. The questions were set by the emperor, and usually related to matters of strategic planning and the art of governance. Candidates' performance was ranked in order of excellence into groups. The top three candidates with the highest scores were in the first group (一甲), and were awarded the titles of Zhuangyuan (狀元 champions), followed by Bangyan (榜眼 first runner-ups), and Tanhua (探花 second runner-ups). These individuals would then be appointed to various offices in the Hanlin Academy where they conducted advanced studies and research while at the same time preparing themselves for the highest ranks in the government bureaucracy. The rest of the crop were awarded the title of Jinshi (進士), and the majority of candidates fell into the second (二甲) or third group (三甲), according to their performance. Many, however, were stuck on the first rung of the provincial examinations for their whole lives. One such example was Hong Xiuquan, the instigator of the Taiping Rebellion.

The quotas for the second and third group were not fixed, and depended on the needs of the government and the decision of the Grand Secretariat and the Council of State, as well as the performance of candidates in a particular year. As a matter of principle, there was every intention to keep the Hanlin Academy slim. From the records, the number of candidates awarded positions in the second and third group seldom exceeded 200 in each category. In the year Wen Su took his examination, 1903, a total of 138 candidates were assigned to the second group, and 174 in the third group, for a total of 312 scholars.

The term Jinshi first appeared in Han (206 BC-220 AD). After Emperor Yingzong of the Ming dynasty, only Jinshis could enter the Hanlin Academy. But not all Jinshis were created equal, and only those candidates deemed to have good potential would be recommended by the Hanlin Academy as Graduate Trainees (Shujishi 庶吉士), who received training in the Jinshi Institute for one year before they officially became Hanlin scholars. Wen Su was appointed as a Shujisi in 1903 after his imperial examination.

The future of a Hanlin depended greatly on his individual character, on the opportunities that presented themselves, and on the perception of his abilities. Those with the highest scores in the examinations might not necessarily have a successful career. Naturally there was also room for office politics at every level within the Academy. Wen Su's position in the palace examination in 1903 was 125th in the second group, and 93rd in the metropolitan examination, while his colleague Hanlin Lai Chihsi came 76th in the same group in the same year, and 251st in his metropolitan examination. The late Communist Party leader Deng Xiaoping had an ancestor named Deng Shimin (鄧時敏 1710-1775) who became a Jinshi during the first year of the era of the Qianlong emperor (1736), having come 89th in the second group.

Details of individual candidates, including those who failed or did not complete the imperial examination, and the names of the presiding examination official, invigilators, assessors, and printing officers were meticulously recorded. All past examination scripts were stored in the cabinet office of the South Study under lock and key. There was no official channel for appeal and cases of review were rare, as they might be seen as a direct challenge to the emperor.

Getting admitted to the Hanlin Academy was no small feat especially when considering the entire population of China at the end of the Qing dynasty was around 440 million. For those from lowly backgrounds, the examination could be a life changer.

Through much of history, remuneration for the Hanlins came in the form of taels of silver and bushels of grain, which was standard practice for all civil servants. In the Qing dynasty, they received between 31 and 180 taels of silver per year according to their rank, while all those who worked in the capital, as all Hanlins did, would receive an additional allowance of between fifteen to ninety bushels of grain, which could be converted to supplementary monetary payments with the same value. By today's standards, the package can only be described as moderate. Even as a senior Hanlin and with his income from his family's landholdings, Wen Su still struggled to make ends meet.

So what was the attraction? While the Hanlins were not well paid, at least they were well-respected. The Hanlin Academy housed a careful selection of the nation's most intelligent men who were seen as important assets to the emperor and the Government. As the nature of their job required, Hanlins were consultants and gave advice on a wide range of subjects, and would have access to many confidential papers. They tended to mingle naturally with senior government officials and ministers during the course of their work; those men, too, had been Hanlins when they began their careers. Some, like Wen Su, would have a chance to meet the emperor and play a role in the real powerhouse of the government. This small and distinguished elite social circle had the authority to make and influence decisions that had an impact on tens or hundreds of millions of ordinary folks. Put simply, it was where the action was.

As the Hanlin Academy was considered to be an office for Hanlins and their associates, all Hanlins had to find accommodation outside for themselves. The wealthier would buy a house nearby, while Wen Su and other Hanlins would stay in hostels in the capital. There was no allowance for accommodation and it was not unusual for junior Hanlins, especially those who came from the same district, to lodge together or near each other.

What exactly did Hanlins do? As an administrative body, the Academy undertook a lot of filing and editorial work in the libraries. Hanlins with the best ranking would normally be assigned the tasks of drafting palace memorials, royal decrees and edicts. Besides their official duties, some would be invited to join various select committees or even the Secretariat, the centre of Government power. An extremely select few would be admitted to the South Study (南書房), an exclusive unit within the Forbidden City where matters of considerable national importance were discussed.

Promotion was a matter of luck and personal preference, but once admitted, Hanlin scholars had to learn the ropes to survive. The exact role of a Hanlin, indeed, was formally "at the emperor's pleasure". Under its grandiose facade, the Forbidden City in those days was not a place for the faint-hearted. Realpolitik was the order of the day and in its dying days, the dynasty's corridors of power was rife with conspiracy, suspicion, and deceit. Some might wonder how Wen Su managed to weather the storm. From his first encounter with emperor Pu Yi, the Hanlin scholar's destiny had been cast and his association with the Qing dynasty ran deep throughout his life. From his humble beginnings as someone who simply wanted to pass examinations and enter the

LOYAL TO THE END

Jinshi Academy, he rose through the ranks and finally, amid all the turmoil and before he realized it, he was offered the position of vice censor-in-chief on the Right of the Censorate (都察院右副都御史) in 1917, a rank of the highest order for non-Manchus in the hierarchy. By then, of course, this was a purely ceremonial post. But Wen Su was sure he was just about to see a revival of the Qing, and he refused to acknowledge the changes, and maintained the fiction that the China outside the doors of the palace had not become a republic.

Wen Su in official attire

WHO IS WEN SU?

Wen Su was born in a small town of Longjiang in Shunde in the Pearl River Delta in January 13, 1879, to a modest family. He had twelve siblings. Born in Longshan with eight other siblings in 1879 and given the name Luen Wai (It should have been eleven, three died before he was born), he mourned the passing of each of them, and at the age of sixty, his only other sibling alive was his widowed elder sister.

For a person of principle who had decided not to follow the mainstream, life would be hard enough, but having a special relationship with the former emperor only made it harder for Wen Su. How could he not realize what people might be saying behind his back? Did he care? He might have been too busy to bother.

While Longjang was small, there was one way in which the town was like no other. It was blessed with lush surroundings, which supported the thriving mulberry tree and fish pond businesses in which Wen's family was involved. Long stretches of political stability and a flourishing economy provided an opportunity for the town to excel in another way—the town boasted a record number of prominent scholars, politicians, and artists, including 90 elite Jinshi scholars and more than 300 provincial graduates, or Jurens (舉人) during the two dynasties of the Ming and the Qing, many of whom have been positively viewed by history. For instance, Wen Rushi (溫汝适 1755-1821), a Jinshi in 1784, was teacher to the Emperor Jiaqing; Wen Chengti (溫承悌), Jinshi in 1820 during the Daoguang reign; Wen Runeng (溫汝能 1748-1811), Juren in 1788 during the fifty-third year of Qianlong's reign; and indeed Wen Su's father, Wen Futing (溫黻廷), who became a Jinshi in 1868 during the seventh year of the Tongzhi reign.

As a child, Wen Su wouldn't have failed to notice the plaque above the main door in the family mansion which read, "Residence of Revenue Minister (司農第). His was essentially a middle-class upbringing, and as a boy, Wen Su probably would have never envisaged a life for himself so deeply entrenched in politics, so dedicated to the Qing empire, and so loyal to the emperor.

He swam almost all his life against the tide of history. From the tender age of seven, Wen Su studied *The Four Books,* the basic Confucian texts, which include the "Doctrine of Great Learning", the "Doctrine of Moderation", "The Analects", and "Mencius". At eight, he read a part of the "Book of Poetry" known as MaoShi 毛詩). At nine he began to tackle the "*I Ching*" (易經), and at ten, he read *Shiji,* the *Book of Historical Records* (史記), and the *Ancient Texts of the Eight Masters of Tang and Song Dynasties.* At eleven, he read *Zuo Zhuan* (左傳). At thirteen, he completed two other key works, the *Wen Zhun* (昭明文選), and the *Rites of Zhou* (周禮).

It was probably in these works that he found his calling. Indeed, he followed a strikingly similar path to that laid out over the centuries, gaining recognition by succeeding within the Imperial examination system, and at the age of twenty-six in 1903, a *gui-mu* year (year of the water rabbit), he became a Jinshi. At twenty-nine, he graduated from the Jinshi Academy and officially became a Hanlin scholar (翰林).

The career of a Hanlin could be hit or miss, and as fate would have it, Wen Su was initially offered a series of junior editorial posts in the Hanlin Academy, the History Library, and the Records Office, followed by elite roles in the government. Given his trajectory, Wen Su certainly must have made an impact at the Hanlin Academy.

When he was in office, Wen Su lived in an alley in Beijing near two mahogany trees. He named his residence Bi Convent (檗庵), referring to the yellowish color of its walls. He then requested fellow Hanlin Jiang Xingcun (1855-1918) to write and make it officially its name, taking in its implications of a life of austerity.

Among the many Hanlin scholars who served the government, Wen Su quickly became noted for his close personal affiliation with the young emperor, and his unwavering loyalty to the Qing monarchy. Years later, to show his devotion to the emperor, he named his first son, born in 1918 only a few years after Pu Yi's abdication in 1912, "Bifu" (必復), which means "must revive". He had six sons in total.

Much has been written in Chinese about Wen Su's superb calligraphy, his mentoring relationship with the young emperor, and his unwavering ambition to revive the Qing dynasty, and these will be covered in this book. His family life, however, has not been well documented, apart from what was recorded in his own chronology of yearly events, which he stopped updating after the death of his cherished daughter, Yu Chiu, in 1928.

He married his wife, Madame Lai, in 1897 when he was aged eighteen. They had two daughters, one of whom died. We also know that Yu Chiu was on her way to becoming a scholar in her own right and that she helped proofread and finalize many of her father's works. He wrote a long and touching obituary for her, of which this is an excerpt:

> "Had you been illiterate and not married so early, your fate might have been different. I am the one responsible!"

LOYAL TO THE END

Overall, however, little is known about the women in Wen Su's life. In 1908, when he was aged twenty-nine and was working in Beijing for the Historiographic Academy (國史館), he took in two mistresses, surnamed Mai and Tang. In 1917, he took in a third, Mistress Su. He wrote often about his wife, but seldom if ever wrote to the woman herself; it wasn't the tradition of the time. But Wen was grief-stricken when she died and wrote a desolate couplet to her. Wen Su later joined another Hanlin scholar, Lai Chi-hsi, in pursuing a teaching career at the University of Hong Kong, and helped in establishing the university's School of Chinese Studies under the Faculty of Arts.

For many years, Wen was in the thick of politics, but it may be a misnomer to cast him as a politician. Nor according to his writings did he have a good impression of politics. He understood how politics bred corruption, and how it often has a tendency to destroy the very foundation of human nature. His views on education may not be readily shared by some, as he took the rather unpopular position that children should not be pampered and should learn to endure hardship. This reminds us of how Alice was ordered "to speak when you're spoken to!" in Lewis Carroll's *Through the Looking Glass* in 19th Century Britain. Today, children's education, or education itself for that matter, has changed in many ways, but the traditional view still has advantages worth considering.

A man of integrity and righteousness, Wen practiced what he preached, and for some, his moral high ground was a hard nut to crack, and could be a nuisance for the uninitiated. Some may criticize Wen for being rigid and inflexible, but others love him for the same reason. Perhaps he was simply a man of his word. Nothing more and nothing less.

THE HISTORY MAN

Much has already been written about Wen as a Hanlin master, as a literary and political figure of the late Qing dynasty, and afterwards as an academic. The focus, however, is often on his unwavering attachment to the Qing imperial cause, his relationship with the last emperor, and his reluctance to come to terms with the idea of reform. How should history judge someone who was loyal to the core, who was passionate about what he believed, and who decided to stand resolute against the tide of history?

Wen Su came under the spotlight at a time when the Qing empire was about to crumble. History, however, put him in a strange and significant position. At twenty-nine as a junior Jinshi, he was summoned to choose a name for the newborn heir-apparent, and two years later he was the one who he himself states placed the child on the throne. Being so close to Pu Yi from such an early age, there was the possibility that this would fix his fate for the rest of his life. But it was not to be.

In 1910, Wen Su was appointed regional governor for Hubei Province, which apparently not only gave him the powers to advise, recommend, and investigate, but also to accuse, condemn, and even impeach others in the bureaucracy. Depending on how you see it as a medium-ranking minister, making allegations against colleagues in the Administrative Court was indeed brave. This was the original purpose of checks and balances in the imperial government system, and Wen clearly was ready to embrace the full import of his job. Therefore, when he saw the deplorable state of social injustice around him and the languishing state of the Qing empire, he knew he had to do something.

In the those few years of the Xuantong reign (1908-1912), Wen Su launched a series of accusations, condemnations, and impeachments against a large number of officials, many with significant imperial backgrounds or connections and holding positions much more senior than himself. Initiating an impeachment in those days was a tedious and lengthy process by today's standards, but it was also rather straightforward. You only needed to collect evidence, prepare a palace memorial (奏摺, documents in an official folder), and present it to the emperor, who at the time was Pu Yi and only five or six years old. In fact, most cases were probably considered by the Prince Regent (攝政王), his father. For many, there were clearly other things to worry about, such as the imminent demise of the Qing dynasty. Some began to run for cover, and others tried to get the most of what could be grabbed during the time remaining.

It is here that Wen saw the ugly side of human nature, and the charges he leveled against other officials ranged from incompetence, fraud, dishonesty, and embezzlement, to corruption, profiteering, conflict of interest, and sheer incompetence. His more notable targets were,

- Zaifeng 載灃, or Prince Chun 醇親王, father of Pu Yi, for professional negligence
- Shanqi 善耆, or Prince Su 肅親王, for indulging in personal

interests
- Yikuang 奕劻, or Prince Qing, First Prime Minister of the Imperial Cabinet, for embezzlement and bribery
- Zaize 載澤, Minister of Finance and Empress Cixi's son-in-law, for misconduct
- Guichun 桂春, Minister of Home Affairs, for professional incompetence
- Ruizheng瑞徵, governor of Huguang Province, for profiteering in property transactions
- Wong Wingbo汪榮寶, Deputy Head of the Law Reform Committee, for misconduct
- Zhu Jiabao, Governor of Anhui Province, for personal misconduct
- Yuan Shikai 袁世凱, first president of Republic of China, for treason.

As Mencius put it, "When I reflect on myself and find myself right, then even if there are tens of thousands in front of me, I would go forward." (*Gong Sun Chou*, part 1) 自反而縮雖千萬人吾往矣 (孟子公孫丑上)

What, if any, were his guiding principles in making the allegations against these important officials? He looked upon the good and the great in history as his role models, and gained inspiration from them. For words of wisdom, he would fall back on the ancient emperors Yao, Shun, Yu, and Tang (堯舜禹湯). He studied the works of past emperors such as Guangxu in *The Imperial Teachings of Dezong* (德宗景皇聖訓). For personal enhancement, he especially liked to read Han Yu (韓愈) and Liu Zongyuan (柳宗元) of the Tang dynasty whose moral values were often explicit in their works. Moreover, he admired the politician Zeng Guofan (曾國藩, 1811-1872) so much that he presented Zeng's writings on effective governance to Emperor

Pu Yi, and even asked his children to copy out his family mottos for reference.

There had been suggestions that Wen Su, whose life evolved for decades within the rarefied world of the imperial court, was oblivious to the world outside and people's suffering. Some would probably conclude that Wen was against reform and the creation of a constitutional government, and that he was not moving with the times. In reality, he was sympathetic to the reformers and revolutionaries, and proposed amnesty for them in court meetings. He was not against a constitutional government, but he was adamant that the proposed framework was half-baked and existed only in form, and instead of the prospect of bringing positive changes, he saw only people rushing around, jostling for votes and positions, and playing politics. It was not his government, it was not anyone's government, it was simply a bunch of charlatans, men for whom lying was second nature. He was sad that the dynasty should have ended only to give birth to such a situation; the nation surely deserved something better.

In an article on Sheng Yun (升允), a loyalist and soldier who was fired for defying a constitutional order, he quoted Mencius as saying, "People are the most important, then the nation, and the sovereign is the least important."

And when quoting from the *I Ching's Great Treatise*, he wrote, "In the Yang trigrams, we have one ruler and two subjects, suggesting the way to an honorable man. In the Ying trigrams, we have two rulers and one subject, suggesting the way to the conceited."

陽一君而二民，君子之道也。陰二君而一民，小人之道也。
(繫辭下卷弟四章)

Following his time as a provincial governor, his life gradually revolved more and more around the young master who was only five at the time of the Xinhai Revolution (1911) which toppled the

Qing. That event ended Pu Yi's reign of just over three years, 267 years of the Manchu Dynasty and 2,000 years of imperial rule.

While many decided to leave the Government, including his close friend and colleague Hanlin Lai Chi-hsi, Wen Su, then thirty-five, who was at that point Acting Investigating Censor for the Sichuan Circuit (四川道), chose to stay with the court. He had probably developed a special compassion for and bond with Pu Yi who could confide in him. And for Wen Su, the child was not only the emperor and his master, but also, he hoped, the future leader of a revived Qing empire.

While China had already become a republic under General Yuan Shikai (袁世凱 1859-1916), inside the Summer Palace, it was basically still business as usual, and work continued on the official biography of the Emperor Guangxu, Pu Yi's predecessor. There was of course no sign of an imminent restoration of the empire, but all the signs are that at this time Wen Su was actively working in collaboration with others to plot such a revival.

This era of Wen's life was filled with setbacks and trials, but his biggest setback came on May 14, 1917, when he was aged thirty-eight. He was on his way to receive his final appointment as Vice-Censor-in-Chief on the Right of the Censorate, a ceremonial gesture aimed at marking the imminent revival of the Qing empire. But he was intercepted en route to Shanghai and forced to turn back, and his plans for a restoration were scuppered.

What was on his mind? At such a time of turmoil and uncertainty, most of his fellow colleagues and ministers would have been most anxious about their own futures. And there were those who decided to jump on the bandwagon in December 1911 when the Empress Dowager Longyu ordered Yuan Shikai to form a provisional constitutional government. But not Ewen Su.

Time passed, his second son Bide was born in 1920 and his third son Bihuo in 1921. Wen must have had mixed feelings when he realized the emperor had grown up – he missed much of it – and invited him to his wedding banquet and celebrations in October 1922. There would probably have been some soul-searching conversations in private moments between them. Would his young man be fit to be a future emperor?

In 1923, Wen Su was summoned to report for duty at the South Study. Wen Su saw this as an opportunity to brief the Xuantong emperor on his possible future role as head of state, and he intended to give the young man strategic lectures on the art of governance based on the notes and palace memorials from Lecture Notes on the Political Summary of Zhenguan (貞觀政要) during Emperor Taizong's reign (626-649) during the Tang dynasty.

When he was appointed to the exclusive South Study, where matters of the highest national importance had always been deliberated, he had the opportunity to access a huge quantity of materials written for the past emperors. These were normally formal advice or recommendations on a wide range of subjects including self-enhancement and effective governance. It began in the second year of Qianlong (1737) when Biyi, the governor of Fengyang Province, proposed that ministers provide input on a daily basis to the emperor with the aim of helping him run the country more effectively. All the documents were kept in proper order in the South Study for future reference.

Many of the numerous tributes and exchanges from his friends before his departure to the South Study in 1923 are included as appendices to this book, providing an important source of first-hand materials for scholars to understand how Wen Su saw his future role with the emperor.

Pu Yi and his entire entourage were forced to leave the Forbidden City in 1924, the year Wen's fourth son Bishen was born. Wen's life changed dramatically as a result. He had spent more than a decade as an attendant to the deposed emperor, but now outside, he found himself living rough and had to sometimes put up with life's adversities.

Gifts and souvenirs from the Xuantong emperor often took the form of luxurious embroidery, a full-length fur overcoat, a royal gilded blanket, a snuff bottle, a plate of lychees, or a plaque adorned with Pu Yi's calligraphy and the imperial seal. To mark Wen's sixtieth birthday in 1937, Pu Yi's royal gift was a plaque bearing the proverb "*ya zhi huai zhen*" (雅志懷貞), meaning roughly "Elegant and Honorable". The prestige attached to the receipt of such presents was something ordinary folks could only dream of, but they did not help Wen pay the rent. Back home in Shunde, in the late 1920s, he had many other things to worry about. His wife, his daughter, his siblings, his relatives, and many of his erstwhile Hanlin cronies, and he himself too, were plagued by ill health. The revival of the Qing empire seemed ever further away, and gradually become a distant illusion. He knew he had to scramble and find a new way to survive.

He went back home to Shunde in 1917—he knew it was time to leave the game of politics. He began building a new home there, which he called the Cuckoo Hut (杜鵑庵). He must have felt shattered and at his lowest ebb and subconsciously cast himself as a tragic character. Over the centuries, Chinese poets have portrayed the cuckoo as a loyal but miserable symbol, which spat blood until its death, yearning for the attention of its master. In the following year, his eldest son was born and was named Bifu (必復), meaning "Must Revive", indicating yet again his passionate loyalty to the Qing empire. In the same year, he also received another concubine, Mistress Wu.

Poets over the centuries have used the cuckoo to symbolize tragedy and even death. But the choice of name for his new home could have been self-mockery or a sign of relief. One of his couplets on the door read:

> 身化衹餘孤卉在，國亡空有百禽哀

> After my incarnation, what's left will only be a lonely flower;
> After the collapse of my country, there will only be the plaintive whining of a hundred creatures.

Another one read:

> 門前今種先生柳，閣道曾看上苑花

Today I grow the master's willows outside the front door, In the past I saw flowers in the corridors of the royal garden.

The master refers to poet Tao Yuanming's (陶淵明, 365-427) created character, "The Biography of Mr Five Willows (五柳先生傳)".

Paraphrasing Tang poet Li Shangyin's (李商隱) "Luxury Qi" (錦瑟), he wrote the following words on completion of his new residence:

> I built this hut and called it Cuckoo,
> No luxury qi and only blame for the years I've been through.
> It's home for your obedience which has turned grey.
> And I owe Your Majesty a formal greeting too.
> 築得茅庵署杜鵑本無錦瑟怨華年幽居臣甫頭今白望帝猶賒一拜虔

The poem explicitly expressed his despair at his fate, as well as his concern for Pu Yi whose fate still hung in the balance. Prior to his trip to Tianjin for his last posting, his friends, peers, and in particular his *'guimu* buddies' (癸卯同年) met and bestowed on him their own poems, and best wishes. For some, it was a trip of no return, as Hanlin Chen Baochen (1848-1935) put it in prose, "Come alive and stronger in the mouth of a lion," and "Lectures are themselves official advice", referring to his daily lectures on *Political Summary of Zhenguan* (貞觀政要) that began in 1925. Inevitably giving advice to the emperor is no inconsiderable art unto itself.

In 1925, Wen Su's daughter Yu Chiu was married to his Hanlin colleague Li Zhanzhi's second son, Tingxun, and Wen was with Pu Yi in the city of Tianjin, where gave the former emperor daily lectures at the Japanese embassy on Tang Dynasty governance. The lectures were supplemented with notes and with "imperial" consent, these notes were published in 1937 under the title of *Lecture Notes on the Political Summary of Zhenguan,* referring to the period under the Emperor Taizong (627-649).

The Tang dynasty (618-907) represents one of the brightest spots in Chinese history, and the name for the period under Emperor Taizong (627-649) chosen by historians, *Zhenguan,* is a flattering term to highlight the excellence of his reign. During his twenty-three years on the throne, this emperor achieved more than any other emperor before him, and the country enjoyed a long period of peace and prosperity as a result. Details of this period were documented and recorded in Wen Su's *A Political Summary of Zhenguan*. In one of the chapters, which certainly was read to Pu Yi, it says that Taizong asked, "What is the secret of being the emperor?" The chancellor and imperial censor Wei Zheng replied, "A good emperor listens widely to all parties, whereas a bad one listens only partially to certain opinions." (*The Way to Good Governance*, Jundo, Vol 1).

Though Wen Su was on the opposite side of the revolutionaries and reformers, he advocated for a surprisingly open approach to how imperial rule should be managed. In a series of reflections on Taizong's reign, he advanced ideas of a moderate, humble, and nuance-minded emperor. He stated: "The emperor and his peole are one unit and are inseperable." Wen Su, in this time of revolutionary political change, was adapting his vision of the monarchy to fit the virtues of the new revolutionary ideals. He emphasized the importance of the individual leader's quality of character over almost any other attribute. If the leader is upright and does not easily give in to temptation then he will be able to navigate the murky grey areas of politics and benefit the nation greatly by doing so. A key virtue for the emperor, according to Wen Su, was his humility. The ability to correctly identify wrongdoing and adjust course promptly was exercised by Taizong repeatedly, and right from the beginning, it was this exact virtue he wanted to instill in Pu Yi. Lastly, Wen Su was not teaching a simplified form of politics to Pu Yi; he also accepted the murkiness of it all. His reflections analyzed the historical course of emperors in balancing nepotism and meritocracy in the imperial system and reflected an understanding that at times nepotism serves to keep key supporters loyal and meritocracy serves to run the government most efficiently. His nuanced and highly adaptable ideas were certainly reflective of a loyal desire to effect the return of Pu Yi to the Dragon Throne.

The lectures continued until 1927 when, for reasons unknown, Wen Su's key collaborator in plans for a restoration, Wang Kuowei, suddenly drowned himself in Kunming Lake, leaving the world with an unsolved case. Fate had taken a sharp turn.

A year later, in 1928, Wen's daughter Yu Chiu died, and he was dealt another blow when his wife Madam Lai passed away a year later. Distressed and disturbed, he knew it was about time to let go.

He finally left Tianjin in 1929 a broken man, mission

unaccomplished, and his vision of a revival of the Qing dynasty dashed. He must have wondered if this gentleman who now introduced himself as Henry was the same toddler he had placed on the throne some twenty years earlier. Unlike his royal cousin Pu Ru (溥儒), Pu Yi didn't seem to take an active interest in anything, much less in once again running his former empire. In spite of this, Wen Su still passionately believed that unlike his predecessor Emperor Guangxu who had lived under Empress Cixi's shadow, Pu Yi should now be his own master; he should be everyone's master! History, however, wasn't playing out according to Wen Su's script.

And so Wen Su went to Hong Kong and followed fellow Hanlin Lai Chi-hsi's footsteps and established an academic career at the University of Hong Kong, where he taught literature and philosophy at the School of Chinese Studies. Over the following years, he produced four volumes of lecture notes on philosophy. Possibly during this time, or perhaps earlier in 1925, he began writing letters home when his son Bifu would have been seven or eight, and intelligent enough to understand and communicate.

His youngest son was born in 1936, just three years before his death in his home in Shunde. Undaunted, he named him Biqing (必清 1937-2005), which meant "Must be Qing", a poetic reflection of his conviction and defiance.

Loyal to the core, the Hanlin could have been, in a parallel strand of history, a kingmaker. His heart was still with the Qing empire, and Pu Yi was his emperor.

Did history do him justice? Perhaps he might not have realized that the political landscape of his time was a far cry from that of the Zhenguan period, and what worked in Tang dynasty wouldn't necessarily work in the China of the 20th Century. Maybe he was not aware that people had changed, from what used to be one-dimensional moral values to a society in which everyone had to compromise. As a firm believer in social justice, he looked at the world at large from the guiding principles of Confucius and Mencius, and believed that all the affairs of humanity could be settled in that way. Can Confucianism change the world of politics? Can Confucianism save the world? That line of thought provides plenty for sociologists and politicians to ponder, even though many would probably conclude that it may not have any relevance in the internet age, or even during Wen's time following the collapse of the Qing dynasty. Confucianism could possibly work today if everyone stood by the teachings of the *Book of Analects*. If our politicians would only start reading the "Classics of Filial Piety" seriously, it could maybe save the world. How could Wen not stay loyal to this scenario, given his background? It was the basis of all he had learned and everything he had done since he was a young boy.

Be that all as it may, sadly, he lived in an era amid world wars when survival and livelihood were the top priorities. His moral values likely put him at odds with many of his colleagues, and eventually he found himself waging a lone battle against almost everyone.

He should perhaps have learned the lessons from the story of how Mencius traveled a thousand miles to see King Hui of Liang who asked if he had anything beneficial he could contribute to his kingdom. In response, the great master said, "Why must we always speak of benefits? What I have is humanism and fairness."

A fighter all his life, Wen's philosophy notes compare traditional Chinese wisdom and Confucianism with Western thought, including Freud's theories and existentialism, and expound his scholarly views on the understanding of Confucian morals, the universe, and existence. He found answers to his questions in these explorations.

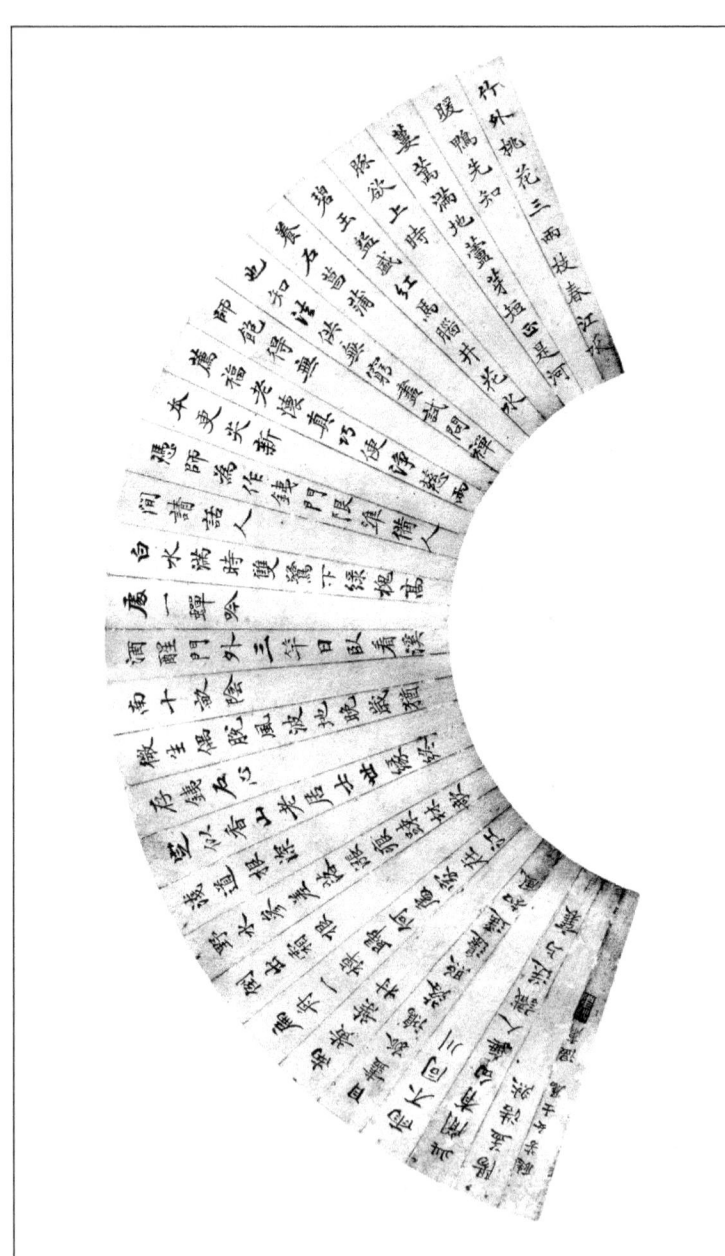

Fan piece by Wen Su for Lai Ditfang (賴棣芳), granddaughter of Lai Chishi and wife of Bifu. Poems by Su Shi, Song poet (1037-1101) (Courtesy Wen Shanglian, son of Bifu)

THE FAMILY MAN

While his public life was often the centre of attention, there has been little mention of the private man in any heretofore published material on Wen Su. As someone who was away from home most of the time, the only means of contact with his family was via correspondence. This was especially so after he moved to Tianjin, when he gave specific instructions for his children to have all his letters properly filed and indexed. Most letters were written to his four sons and sometimes they were meant to be read together. He also wrote to Yu Chiu (如昭), his third and most adored daughter who, as mentioned before, was married to the son of Li Zhanzhi, his fellow Hanlin, in 1925. Very few letters, however, were addressed to his wife, Madam Lai, but nevertheless she was often mentioned in other letters.

Was he a happy man? On his sixtieth birthday in 1937, he wrote an article for his sons. He drew parallels between himself and late Qing politician Zhang Zhidong (張之洞 1837-1909) whose birthday fell in June and received a couplet which was made up of titles of the ancient *Book of Poetry* (詩經). One of them was Jianghan (江漢), and every time he read it, he was touched. Wen said if they wanted him to be happy, they could simply pick any of these poems and recite it before him, and he would drink after each verse until he finally got drunk. That was a way to filial piety, he wrote at the end of the piece.

Bifu (必復), the second child and eldest son, took after his father especially in his interest in literature. Though he was only a few years older than his younger brothers, he acted as a fatherly figure and looked after them when their father was not home, as was the case most of the time. When his sister Yu Chiu got married, he was only seven; when he married in 1935, she had already passed away. Wen Su's joyous couplet on the main door of the home on his son's wedding read:

> In all luxuries, everyone gives us their blessings, laughing at my zaniness, And I'm grateful to my ancestors for living up to the description in Han Yi (a part of the Book of Poetry).
> With willows and plums everywhere, it's the day before the winter solstice
> So get yourselves drunk, and teach your kids to go for the Duling Cup Challenge.

娶長媳大門喜聯
金荃玉鏡群公備錫嘉言笑我漸癡聾鑽祖幸承韓奕句岸
柳山梅此日剛逢小至勸君須酩酊教兒亦覆杜陵盃

Composing poems or couplets like this, often with rigid linguistic requirements, could be done at the spur of the moment by most Hanlins. It is an exquisite literary skill only acquired over many years, or even decades.

Considering his lengthy periods away from home, how does Wen Su measure up as a father? Reading Wen Su's correspondence with his children, both sons and daughter, feels like going through a course on liberal studies and social science. Their intimate exchanges also shed light on the other side of a politician, and his real character can be seen from this perspective. Whether he was writing about uncertain political situations, family issues, his children's behavior, or the proper attitude to studying, he did not mince his words. He might have been strict in his approach, but Wen Su was clearly very concerned about his children and their education. In one particular letter to Bifu, he discussed specifically how to practice calligraphy, and lashed out at Bifu's younger brothers for not doing it properly. In others, he would talk about the political theories of Mencius, or the poetry of Han Yu and Liu Zongyuan, or perhaps Zeng Goufan's admirable moral character.

He was much more passionate in his letters to Yu Chiu, his daughter and the eldest among them, who was always understanding and considerate. His couplet to mark the significance of Chiu's wedding is a good example. In line with the traditions of the literati, the couplet makes substantial references to historical events to imply his blessings for daughter Ah Chiu. The first line refers to a father who wanted to find a home and husband for his daughter Ji, and happily found Han (from the Hanlin). The second line made reference to the legendary figure Zhou Yu (175-210) of The Three Kingdoms, and the father who chose him as his son-in-law.

季女于歸大門喜聯韓姞相攸
敢方蹶父喬公選婿喜得周郎

When the news of his daughter's death reached him in 1928, Wen Su could not hide his emotions and broke down uncontrollably. He was dealt another blow a year later when his wife Madam Lai died. He penned this couplet of remembrance in her honor:

> You struggled to stay alive to wait for my return,
> but why didn't you leave a word?
> You were optimistic despite life's shortcomings,
> but would weep for our kids.

哭亡室黎夫人聯忍死待吾歸何無片語
留身後達觀看世厭卻為諸離一涕零

Bitter but passionate, love is strongly evident through the words. Fate, however, seemed to have put him on the wrong side of things. His eldest son was then only eleven, the youngest, Bixin, was hardly five, and his last son Biqing was not yet born.

The letters included in this book were mostly written between the late 1920s and the mid-1930s when the boys were only in their early teens. The children were Yu Chiu 如昭 (1908-1928), Bifu 必復 (1918-1985), Bida 必達 (1920-?), Biguo 必果 (1921-?), Bixin 必信 (1924-196?), and Biqing 必清 (1936-2006).

Among them, Bifu was over the following years probably most well-known within the Hong Kong's teaching profession and the Chinese classical literature community. In his various teaching undertakings, from Clementi Middle School to the Evening School of Higher Chinese Studies and Shue Yan College (now Shue Yan University), he went by the name Wan Chunghan (溫中行) and was well respected within the profession. Most of his students or colleagues, however, did not realize that his father was Wen Su, the famous Hanlin scholar. Today, some graduates might still recall with affection the master in a cheongsam who could recite *Zuo Zhuan* (左傳) in its entirety. With his extraordinary mental resources, he was always ready to finish a classical poem or couplet without missing a beat.

Bixin's life was a tragic personal statement against communism. He went by the name Wei Han (惠行) and taught in a primary school in the town of Rongqi (容奇) in Guangdong Province. In 1958, he pledged his father's letters and other documents to a trusted friend, who worked as head teacher in the same school. It was the year of the Great Leap Forward in China, soon followed by the Cultural Revolution. Bixin was probably aware that his background could possibly make him the target of persecution by the Red Guards and he jumped to his death in a pond nearby before the revolution could get him.

Bida and Biguo's lives were not fully documented and they slipped into oblivion in people's memories.

Biqing, the youngest among the siblings, did not follow his father's footsteps and enjoyed a life outside the literary community. However, his ownership of his father's works and mementoes also meant he was associated with Hok Hoi Library, the famous study hall that Wen Su and other Hanlin scholars established in 1923 with the objective of advancing understanding of Chinese culture. Now, almost a century later, the tradition is still very much kept alive. And this, if nothing else, is something Wen Su should be proud of. The rest is history.

*Photo with Chen Tsedian, left, and Yao Yun, (姚筠1841-1927), right
(Photo courtesy of Tsai Kingyan)*

FRIENDS, HANLINS, & THE CONNECTIBLES

Written records of Wen Su's acquaintances outside Hanlin and the palace are scarce, and most of his lifelong friends were from the Hanlin Academy, in particular the few who qualified as Jinshi in the same year, whom he fondly referred to as his "*guimu* (癸卯 or colleagues). They included, among others, Lai Chi-hsi 賴際熙, Au Fei-wu 區徽五, Li Zhanzhi 黎湛枝, and Shang Yanzhen 商衍瀛. Indeed, Li and Lai later became his in-laws as his eldest son Bifu (必復) married Lai's granddaughter, and Li's son tied the knot with Chiuyu, his third daughter. He and Lai later both taught at the University of Hong Kong.

Pu Yi probably looked upon Wen Su as his mentor as they had forged a strong bond. While everyone had to perform the ritual of "kneeling thrice and bowing nine times", there were times when Pu Yi ignored this protocol in private.

Pu Yi was born a Manchu noble, and protocol required that he keep his distance from commoners, yet on many occasions he actually took the initiative to break this barrier. In 1923, he admitted Wen to the prestigious South Study as his personal adviser with the prestigious but strange title of 'South Study Walkabout'. Here Wen gave many lectures to the emperor on the art of good governance. There were moments of optimism and hope for a return to the monarchy, and outside the Study, the government was just as corrupt as ever. But while his passion might have been real, but his dream was unattainable.

On one occasion in 1923, a year before his forced abdication, Pu Yi summoned Wen Su to Yanxindian (養心殿) and said, "I have heard you write poems. Do you have copies? You may present them to me. Since you're already working here (in the South Study), let me know anytime you want to talk, or send me an official request folder (具摺陳奏)."

And in 1926, when Wen Su submitted an official proposal on the revival of sovereignty, Pu Yi said, "I often haven't realized my mistakes. Your proposal touches my heart, and I will keep it with me and read it day and night to correct my past errors. From now on if you have any ideas, just come and speak to me and correct me."

His last official message to the Xuantong emperor in 1939 was in effect his last will and testament in which he blamed himself for not being able to serve any more and wishing Pu Yi and his empire a glorious future. It was officially presented in court by his son, Bifu. Excerpts of it read as follows:

> "... I understand I have reached the twilight of my life. Now we are miles apart and I'm not able to see you. My word and tears seem further away. I hope Your Majesty will take good care of yourself and wait for God's intention. Pay attention to details and observe the world at large, just like Shaokang of ancient Guan (Xia dynasty, BC 1912-1972), or emperor Guangwu who revived the Han dynasty (Eastern Han 25-220). Then although I may have gone, my spirit will still be with you.

I am instructing my second son to dictate this will memorial and present it later.
From your faithful obedient servant
Ji-mu year (1938) November 20

"...自知此生已在旦暮,而君門萬里,瞻就無從。言與淚皆神隨心遠。伏願皇上遵時養晦,靜待天心。事物之細微,觀時會之遠大。以少康之綸邑,致光武之中興。則臣雖死之日,猶生之年。謹口授遺摺,命臣次子繕呈。伏乞皇上聖鑒。
謹奏 己卯年十一月二十日

There were other more senior ministers around the former emperor, but Wen clearly enjoyed a very special relationship with him.

Outside this close-knit circle, one of his most prominent friends was Chen Zidan (陳子丹), a wealthy merchant and philanthropist with a flare for poetry and literature and who mixed comfortably with the Hanlin masters. Wen was first introduced to him in 1912 by Lai on a trip to Hong Kong. They became very close friends, so much so that they pledged that should one of them pass away before the other, the survivor should write the other's obituary. Indeed, Lai also once made a similar pledge with Chan, that it should not be left to others.(1)

孰為後死當為先撰狀斯可傳信更不可假諸人也

Well as fate would have it that Chen and his *guimu* colleagues all passed away before Wen Su, and he was left with the task of writing their obituaries.

In Chen's obituary, he wrote:

"... I recall our friendship was much enhanced through Lai (Chi-hsi). Whenever the three of us met, we'd

surely have a drink and started talking nonsense and things, often bursting into laughter. When there was someone else present, you would just keep silent but wouldn't display any signs of subservience. You were easygoing, but nevertheless you remained true to your principles. As I'm now very much a refugee here and short of resources, you were always there to help. At first I thought your generosity was only for your friends, but as I observed, you were always there helping others during natural disasters, or promoting civic duties..."
(Obituary for Chen Tzedian, 1934. *From Anthology of Collected Works,* Wen Su)."

And a couplet mourning his passing reads:

小別經年何期病已彌留後至幸逢元伯面論文卅載要說
貧能知我並時孰似叔牙賢
We haven't met for a year. How could it be that you're near the end of life! You are like Yuen Ba, and I'm fortunate to know you. We've been discussing poetry for some twenty years. I'm so poor but you know me well, and you are like Shu Ya, always helping me.

In his preface to the posthumous publication of *Anthology of Poetry* by Wen Su, Zhang Cikong 張賜康 (1873-?) wrote:

Alas! These are poems left by the Honourable Wen Su. Compared to Juan Er (卷耳, one of the poems in the preface to the Ancient Book of Poetry) (6) they are even more touching, and more memorable. Wen and I had been great friends, and were particularly close during our late years. I often stayed at his Cuckoo Hut once every ten days, and found that he always had Lu You's (7) *Collected Works* on his desk, and realized he shared the same passion with someone centuries before him. His greatest regret in life was not being able to see his country united. I am poor at poetry, but Wen was an acclaimed poet, and he would often choose my works for discussion. He once said with resentment, "Why should I wish to leave a name for my poetry? My deeds, and my beliefs, are recorded in the palace memorials and lecture notes. Those who know me should be here. And those who mourn me should also be here..."

(Excerpt from Preface to Anthology of Poetry by Wen Su, 檗庵詩集)

He was particularly close to fellow Hanlin scholar Li Zhanzhi perhaps because of their in-law relationship. He also appeared to be much more relaxed in his tone in their exchanges, in stark contrast to his rather restrained approach in court that his office required. This is understandable, as once out of office, albeit only physically, he was free to speak his mind. In his correspondence with Li, he displayed his nuances in the language with a good sense of humor.

He felt a great sense of camaraderie with certain Hanlins from the past. Wen was particularly attracted to the personal life of Chen Gongyin (陳恭尹), alias Chan Dulu (陳獨漉 1631-1700), a Ming dynasty poet and politician whose works had a profound influence on the Lingnan school of poets during the Qing dynasty. Chen was noted for his utter loyalty to the Ming throne, an honorable character which must have inspired Wen and spiritually linked them together. But if there was anything in common between them, it would have been Longshan, their homeland in Shunde County in southern China. In 1919, in an act of appreciation and remembrance, Wen Su renovated the grave of Chen, compiled *The Longshanian* (龍山鄉志), printed a supplement to Chen's literary works, wrote an obituary for him, and edited his chronicles, all at his own expense.

"Like the dying falcon, we're in different dynasties, but our misery is the same. I'll use soil to strengthen your funeral memorabilia," he wrote.

He might often have been financially strapped, but Wen Su was constantly in the company of the rich and famous. In 1928, philanthropist and entrepreneur Kan Hungchiu (簡孔昭) of Nan Yang Tobacco Co Ltd donated land and money for the construction of the Confucius Hall on Caroline Hill, Hong Kong. In recognition of this act of generosity, Wen Su presented him with an unfinished imperial examination script taken in 1847 by the Jinshi Zhu Ciqi (alias Zhu Jiujiang 朱九江 1807-1882). Wen Su could not have known him, of course, but obviously he was inspired by Zhu's integrity as a scholar. The script had leaked from a store room in the Cabinet Office during the early days of the Xuantong reign, and changed hands in the market before Wen acquired it.

It has been more than a century since Zhu took his examinations. He didn't make it to the Hanlin Academy, but his script became world famous. Could these two men have been connected somewhere in another world?

It cannot have been all work and no play. What did he and other Hanlin scholars do in their spare time? One of the popular activities was attending literary or poetry gatherings (雅集) where their profound academic talents were put to good use. Indeed, there was no shortage of like-minded intellectuals in the work place. It was on one such occasion when Wen first met Chen Tzedian in Hong Kong. These wise men created new rules for a game to make it more demanding and enjoyable, and one of the spin-offs was the time-honored "poetry challenge" (詩鐘), in which participants were required to complete a poem, or a couplet, or add to an existing one within the time limit set, usually within the complete burning of an incense stick. Their works might not be readily comprehensible by today's standards as they made extensive reference to the classics even though this was not an official requirement and their poems were usually done on the spur of the moment. The fruit of these challenges often reflected their mentality of despair and confusion. On one of these occasions, Wen wrote:

退之憤世成師說
回也冥心學坐忘
Han Yu resents the world and writes a piece on teaching,
Yan Hui meditates and learns to forget the adversities in life.

Han Yu (韓愈), a Tang poet, was renowned for his righteous and argumentative styles in his writing, while the part about Yan (顏回), a student of Confucius', was inspired by Zhuang Zi (莊子).

These gatherings attracted a significant following from the endangered species of classically trained scholars, and generations after the original Hanlin scholars passed away, the tradition is still very much alive today in various shapes and forms. The fun, however, can only be fully understood within these limited communities.

In a speech probably made in 1928, prepared for the University of Hong Kong's Chinese Society at its inauguration, Wen said in closing, "... Poetry is about making your own statement... Wu Weiye (吳梅邨) was unmatched in his talents, but was not accepted during his time. His honorable character was reflected in his prose. He was accurate and sharp in his narrative and arguments, and that's why his works are such epics."

This reads like an argument to end all arguments, and what better way to put a stamp on the universal principles of humanity! Wen may have been talking about poetry, but he was indeed also talking about life.

Has history misjudged him, or had he misjudged history? Here is a man who would stand up to the highest morals, without fear or favor. Here is a man who could have changed the course of history. And here is a man who has long been misunderstood. Who was the other Wen Su? Friend, mentor, romantic, and above all, a family man. Despite the promise of glory for a life in high office, Wen finally chose a different path. But for him, it was too little, too late.

THE LETTERS MAN

During his long career in politics, first in Beijing and later in Tianjin from 1924, Wen's home was often a home away from home, which meant leaving wife Madame Lai in Shunde. Yu Chiu, the eldest daughter whom he affectionately called Ah Chiu or Chiuyi, probably stayed with him in the capital most of the time. Bifu, the eldest son, was born in 1918, and was hardly seven when sister Chiuyi was married in 1925. During his absence, Wen maintained communication with his family via correspondence, mainly addressed to Bifu. It would be reasonable to deduce that he began his continuous stream of letters in the late 1920s when his eldest son was at least old enough to understand, and able to engage in any meaningful conversations with him. Perhaps distance makes one mature faster. In any event, Bifu became a precocious boy growing up in his father's shadow and apparently became a child prodigy in his early teens.

In keeping with the concepts of distance learning and continuous education, the contents of these letters often went well beyond simple exchanges of personal and family business, and many of them were anything but personal. Philosophical thoughts of Confucius and Mencius were often tossed around and discussed meticulously against real life. So were the works of Han Yu and Liu Zongyuan of the Tang dynasty, two of Wen's favorite past masters. Subjects of interest range from the proper way to approach calligraphy, analysis of the styles of different classic works, and ways to enhance oneself and be spiritually close to the great masters. On calligraphy, Wen would explain in minute detail how to practice, how to properly 'read' a master's scripts, and even how to choose writing brushes. While on writing, he would explain what makes certain writings great, the art of how to reference the classics, and why focus was important. Indeed, many of his comments, written almost a century ago, are still perfectly valid by today's standards.

One of the questions teachers, especially language teachers, are frequently asked is simply how to write a good piece of work. While most examination authorities set their own guidelines, they invariably focus on the three major areas — content, language, and organization. But it is ultimately the overall impression created which sets apart the best from the above-average, and the above-average from the mediocre. The best candidates are always those whose writings can engage readers' interest and inspire them to think. Wen might not have been aware of these instrumental terms, but his holistic approach in judging his sons' letters candidly fits into these categories. However, discussing the rather complex issues of neo-classicism, or the massive literary contributions of the Tang poet Han, or the political treatise of Zeng Guofeng could be a bit too much for the children at times.

Wen Su was clearly serious about his letters to his sons, and was equally so about the letters from his sons. He made clear the requirements they had to observe, including a proper filing system, which had all the letters indexed. He also stressed the importance of proper language register, protocol, and correctness in their choice of words. On one occasion, he lashed out at his son's inappropriate use of terms which should better be reserved for peers; and on another, he criticized Bifu for content which was not considered relevant when writing to his senior.

One may perhaps be baffled by his rather pessimistic views of his family's financial situation considering his official remuneration as a Hanlin. In some of his letters he lamented at the thought of finding better times, though they were comparatively well-to-do. Sometimes, he would transfer money home with his letter and ask Bifu to settle debts. The Wen family were landlords and had tenants who rented their lands for farming or other businesses. It was not a stable income and when there was a poor harvest, bad days would be upon them. Wen was at the helm of the family business after all his brothers passed away, and he felt obliged to take care of everything, thus putting himself under enormous pressure.

For much of his working life, the Hanlin scholar relied heavily on letters to keep tabs on his family. Understandably he required them to write at least once a week in a fixed format, and he received a continuous stream of letters from his three sons. By the mid-1930s even Bishen, the youngest among them, was intelligent enough to correspond with him. For any average father, reading these letters should have been a definite source of pleasure, and watching the accomplishments of his family acrue, a bonus. But when from time to time he found that the children did not live up to his expectations, his words could be downright harsh, and at one point, he resorted to creating a study timetable for Biguo.

Of course, family letters are not palace memorials where you know when you should exercise the art of diplomacy. His letters to his sons adhered to a rather rigid pattern, and he also expected them to follow in kind. He was strict in his overall tone, but somehow his love for his wife and children filtered through the pages. In a way his approach might seem a bit authoritative. For instance, when addressing his sons, he would invariably adopt a word with an overwhelming undertone, "yu" (諭), which means an order, and which also effectively makes clear the conversation was not a level-playing field. When referring to their letters to him, he would choose the word "ben" (稟), which implies they were talking to someone in a respectable position, by virtue of being their father.

It was also fascinating to note the names of people he mentioned in these letters, most of them Hanlin scholars. They include Chen Baito (陳伯陶), Cen Guangyue (岑光樾), and Li Zhenzhi (黎湛枝). Chen Tzedian (陳子丹) was also mentioned in a letter about Bida's education. These people formed a closed community among themselves. And as it turned out, Wen outlived all of them and was sadly obliged to take up the task of writing their obituaries and epitaphs.

Letters came and went, and so did the people involved. There were no records as to how or why the cycle of chain letters ended. Could it have been a change in the family situation? Bida was sent to Hong Kong to study, possibly in the mid-1930s. Wen also had to accept that Biguo was not too keen on academic studies, and his last son Biqing was only three when Wen died.

These letters opened my eyes; they also opened my heart.

Our honorable man of letters might never have considered that this set of family correspondence would ever have any opportunity to come to light decades after his time, and be read by historians and academics, and others. The various implications and conclusions derived from these letters are not intended to be definitive or authoritative. Yet behind each and every piece there lies a story — the story of a man both ordinary and extraordinary.

林前都察院副都御史通家愚弟溫肅頓首拜書
翰林院編修通家弟區大典翰林院編修通家弟岑光樾翰林院檢討通家弟區大原度支部主事通家弟羅汝楠河南即用知縣通家弟陳煜庠湖北候補道愚弟金湛霖文科學士通家弟李景康文科學士通家弟林棟世愚弟宋寶琳同頓首拜祝

昔

歲在屠維大荒落壯月

穀旦

廣州 龍山鄉

侍御第

憑必達

杜織

光生收入

廿四廢年十一号
廿八日接到第十号

CAPTION

FAMILY LETTERS

書法但求不俗此不善書者之言也不俗二字豈易言哉必胸有羅吳卷碑版博覽乃能不俗近世如沈子培王靜庵字多誤不俗矣究不能謂之善書也

FRANCIS WANN

LETTER 1
Excerpt from Wen Su's Letter to Bifu
(ON CALLIGRAPHY)

The remark that calligraphy has to be unique must have come from a novice. "Uniqueness" itself is something easier said than done. One needs to have studied tens of thousands of scripts and tablets before attaining that level. Works of contemporaries such as Shen Zepui (沈子培 1850-1922) or Wang Jing'an (alias Wang Guowei (王國維 1877-1927) may be considered unique, but not necessarily masterly.

書法但求不俗，此不善書者之言也。不俗二字豈易言哉！必胸羅萬卷碑版博覽，乃能不俗。近世如沈子培王靜庵字可謂不俗矣，究不能謂之善書也。

達果寄來臨帖兩頁、其筆意固不類古人所字
樣、亦毫無類似此、且鈔帖而非臨帖也、前人
臨帖之法、須先將其文念熟、如醉翁亭記宜從環滁皆
山起念到底、庶後歐曾之意
然後逐字細看、看到忽起合著眼想得出那
個字模樣來、然後下筆背臨、畢乃攤
出該帖來對勘、有不合處下記著下次臨時
改正、如此方是臨古、否則帖自帖、我自我、雖鈔
一萬遍、何益哉、後覩照此清
也、

FRANCIS WANN

LETTER 2
Calligraphy to Li Kungman (李孔曼)

Received two pages of calligraphy from Da and Guo. The brush strokes made no reference to the masters, and even its form was not similar. It was only copying and not studying the scripts. Doing it properly would, according to our masters, require a thorough understanding of the whole piece. (For example, in an account of "The Drunken Man's Booth" (醉翁亭記)[1], you will have to begin from "the mountains surrounding him" to "Loliang Ouyang Xiu", then read every word in detail until you are so fluent that you can conjure up the shape of the word with your eyes closed. Then dictate it from memory. Afterwards, compare it against the master script. Take note of any irregularities, and correct them the next time. That is what we call learning from the past masters. Otherwise the script is here, and you're there. Even if you've copied ten thousand times, what is the point?

Son Fu, you should also follow this when you do the "Preface to the Imperial Instructions".[2]

達果寄來臨帖兩頁。其筆意固不類古人，即字樣亦毫無類似。此直是鈔帖而非臨帖也。前人臨帖之法，須先將其全文念熟，（如醉翁亭記宜從　［環滁皆山］　起念到　［廬陵歐陽修也］）然後逐字細看，看到熟極，合着眼想得出那個字模樣來，然後下筆背臨。臨畢，乃攤出該帖來對勘。有不合處，　記着。下次臨時改正；如此方是臨古。否則帖自帖，我自我。雖鈔一萬遍，何益哉！復兒臨聖教序亦宜照此法也。

---

1 Zùiwēngtíng 《醉翁亭記》"An Account of the Drunken Man's Booth" is a semi-autobiographical essay by Ouyang Xiu (1007-1072). The title refers to himself and the Zuiweng Pavilion (Zuiwengting) near Chuzhou City, Anhui.(1) The essay's most well-known line is: The Drunken Man cares not for the wine, his interest lies in the landscape (醉翁之意不在酒，在乎山水之間也), an idiom still used in modern Chinese to describe someone with an ulterior motive.
2 Chu Siuliang, Tang politician and calligrapher (596-658)

孟子恆心恆產說此有何難解有恆產者有恆心即
衣食足而禮義興之說也無恆產者無恆心即
之教死惟恐不贍矣掛禮義教之說也此若賢君
制民之產而言富而後能教也
去年雖購得孟子要略一書尺一冊汝可檢出書籍內
細讀其中分心性手道芽類讀之易得端緒有不
明白處取朱子集註一看便瞭然矣此書朱
子所編篡此書後學禮之固便於了解即宿學
作序奏此書後學禮之固便於了解即宿學
讀之亦便以更提綱挈領最賅括也

年　月　日

FRANCIS WANN

LETTER 3

Why is it so difficult to understand Mencius' theory on property? Those with property are those with will. That's why they say "Meat is much, but manner is more." Those without property are also without desire. As Mencius said, "When they have no means to survive and to take care of their parents, how can they have time for etiquette? A good emperor will require his subjects to own property. Only when you are affluent, can you talk about education."[3]

Last year, I bought the book *A Concise Summary of Mencius* in one volume. You can pick it out and read it (in the Classics cabinet). It covers topics such as ethics and governance. You may get inspired by reading it. Refer to Explanatory notes from Zhu Xi[4](朱子集註) if necessary. This Summary was originally edited by Zhu Xi, but had fallen into disrepair and later was re-edited by Liu Sukwen[5] with a preface by Zeng Guofan. It's easy for beginners but is just convenient for seasoned scholars as it's excellent in outlining the essential principles.

孟子恆心恆產數語，此有何難解？有恆產者有恆心，即衣食足而禮義興之謂也。無恆產者無恆心，即下文《民之救死，惟恐不贍，奚暇持禮義哉》之謂也。此為賢君制民之產而言。富而後能教也

去年新購得《孟子要略》一書及一冊，汝可檢出（在經部書箱內）細讀。其中分心性王道等類，讀之易得端緒。有不明白處，取《朱子集註》一看便瞭然矣。此要署本朱子所編，後殘闕不全，經劉椒雲重輯，曾文正作序。此書淺學讀之固易於了解，即宿學讀之亦便，以其提綱挈領最賅括也。

---

3   Mencius (372 BC-289 BC). Text from Teng Wen Gong (volume 1)
4   Zhu Xi 朱熹 (1130-1200) Song dynasty calligrapher, historian, philosopher, poet, politician and editor. Influential in the development of neo-confucianism.
5   Liu Sukwen (劉椒雲 1818-1849). Juran (candidate for imperial examination) in 1840, official in Imperial Academy.

古來名文無有定格文成法立在當日作者忘不知矣所以教後人為當請師計不説以精妙不另以題其體若學者依其所説皆者文則一世不會作文矣況問逆秦與抆佢少卿上此較氣勢此乃外行話凡文有體論与書出體並論且抆佢少卿上係憤懣不平一類非氣勢渾顥一類也

凡讀古文必韓柳皆須將其全集流覽一遍且必須看註知其生平行事与其交遊之人眡述所並後讀其文方有興味玉括評語雖多得當

御批則不可不讀益人者甚少 若唐宋文醇之

有註

家有東雅堂刻韓集及孫評柳集均

池好讀玉穎送窮語其易曉此遊戲文也駢神智不少也
體文鈔末一類最多此種文不妨一覽以悟其趣

FRANCIS WANN

LETTER 4

There have never been any rules for great writing. Rules come from writing. The great writers themselves probably had no idea during their time. Yet those after them who wanted to be teachers or lecturers would like to talk about the wonderful rules, otherwise they were not able to convince others of their capabilities. If students follow them, they can never write!

You asked how we compare the momentum between *Crimes of Qin* and *Responding to Yam Shaoqing*. It's a question from an outsider. All writings have structure, and how can you compare an argument to a letter? Moreover, the "Yam" one is littered with personal grudges, and not written with strong rhetoric and arguments.

When you read the classics such as those of Han or Liu, you must first read their whole collections once (we have the block-printed version of Han's anthology from Tung Ngai Tong and Critique of Liu's works by Sun Wei (孫琮)[6], all with explanatory notes), and you should also read the explanatory notes about their lives, friends, and the places they had been to. This should make reading their works more interesting. Reviews are plenty, but quality ones are rare. Remarks from Tang and Song emperors are must-reads, as they are often stimulating and uplifting. You like works such as Mao Ying's "Biography" and "Poverty" because they're easy. These are writings for amusement. There are plenty in *Collection of Parallel Prose*. You may just read them for fun.

古來名文無有定格，文成法立，在當日作者亦不知其所以然。後人為當教習、當講師計，不說得精妙不足以顯其能。若學者依其

---

[6] Sun Wei (孫琮). Collector, writer, literatus in late Ming and early Qing dynasties. Self-proclaimed hermit.

所說法為文，則一世不會作文矣！

汝問《過秦論》與《報任少卿書》比較氣勢，此乃外行話。凡文有體，論與書安能並論！且報任少卿書係憤鬱不平一類，非氣勢渾灝一類也。

凡讀古文如韓如柳，皆須將其全集流覽一遍（家有東雅堂刻韓集及孫評柳集。均有註），且必須看註以知其生平行事與其交遊之人蹤迹所經之地，然後讀其文方有興味。至於評語雖多，得當者甚少，若唐宋文醇之 御批則不可不讀，益人神智不少也。汝好讀《毛穎送窮》等文，謂其易曉，此遊戲文也，《駢體文鈔》末一類最多此種文，不妨一覽以博其趣。

FRANCIS WANN

LETTER 5
To Son Fu, etc,

Mail No 7 was dispatched here on 6th, and I guess it has arrived. I haven't received any of yours since No 4. Should be on the way, I suppose. Got a letter from Lokchi the day before which said he asked Mr Chung to take HK$100 to Hong Kong, and I guess it's been received by now. Another HK$100 will also be brought back by Lokchi in one or two days. This HK$200 can be exchanged for more than $280 in silver currency. With this, we can then return the money we borrowed from your sixth aunt, and it should also see us through until August or September (It should also help pay the twelve taels deposited with Houyutang co-operative on behalf of Baoqiongtang). You guys never realize how difficult life is! Even with rental income, we still need to struggle to make ends meet for most of the year. I just can't imagine what life is like during famine with no rental income!

諭復兒等：此間初六日發弟七號回，計已達。來稟自弟四號後，未見讀到，想在途中耳。前日接到樂之來函，云於六月初五交鍾生帶回港紙一百員，此時想已收到矣。大約日內尚有一百員亦由樂之轉回。有此二百員港幣，可易毫銀二百八十餘員。可還六嬸借款，並可支持到八、九月（報瓊堂應供厚畬堂會十二兩亦在此項內提供）。汝等未知度日之難。有租收尚且要捱大半年，饑荒無租收，則更不堪設想矣。
　　六月十六日 父字弟八號。

諭復兒知此間初六日裝革匕號回計已達
未審何萬四號後未見續到想在途中耳
前日接到樂之來函云於六月初承支鍾生帶
回港紙一百員此時想已收到矣大約日內當
有一百員出由樂之特囬有此二百員港幣可
易毫銀二百六十餘員可還六嬸借款並可支
持到八九月 拟瓊堂庭供厨會堂會 汝等未知度日之
十三兩亦在此項內提供
難有租收尚且要捱大半年餘兄無租收則
更不堪設想矣
六月十六日父字 第八號

FRANCIS WANN

LETTER 6

Some of Juilong's rent for the first quarter is still not settled, and will be transferred to the Yujintong public account. Make sure he clears the amount in the final quarter, and check the books to see the amount outstanding. The other rental receivables from lands and fields such as Juilong Foundation, Hoisumsa fenced field, Pok Cheung, and Hoisumsa Sakwat must list out the names of the proprietors so uncle Koonman can go after them.

When reading collected works, you would need to categorize and edit them according to their nature. That's what the beginners say or otherwise they cannot memorize. Now is the right time for you. When your writing has developed into passages, you'll have to polish it, and refer to the classics for enhancement. The deeper you go the more elegant it becomes. At that time, don't bother about a word or a sentence, or try to imitate or copy others. Try to ponder over the word "jait" (澤) in the phrase "Learning from the classics" (澤古) and you would understand what it means.

I haven't started my work yet. I don't really know what they say, but it's all rumors. There are some old copies of Chiu Yin Daily in the cabinet for South China Literary Works. Pick out those marked with red circles which cover news of Jehol and send them here. The articles are short and can be included in one letter. June 21. No 9

…聚隆頭季租尚有些欠，撥歸畲經堂公家收。將來交尾季租時要他找清方可。查收租簿便知所欠多少矣。其他各沙田應交之租如石沙，如聚隆基壆，如博漿，如海心沙圍田，如海心沙沙骨皆宜列出引耕人姓名與冠文公，俾其代催問也。

讀文選將其碎錦分類纂鈔。此為初學作詞章者言。不如是則不能記憶。汝現在為此正其時矣。至文章既成片段之後，須工益求工。必澤古深，乃能古雅，斯時則不在乎一句一字之未摹擬剽

聚隆頭李祖尚有些欠擬滙會經墾此前收穫未
查尾季祖附要他找清查收租便知所欠多少矣
名沙冒應支之祖如石沙如眾隆基墾如博樂如海
心沙坦圍田如海心沙、骨皆宜列出引耕人姓名與
冠文伏俾父代催問也
讀文選將文碑錦分類纂鈔必為初學作詞章者
言不妨是則不能記憶汝現在為此正是時矣玉文孝
既成片段之後須工益求工必澤古深乃能古雅斯
時則不在乎一句一字之未摹擬剽竊也玩澤古澤今
便能領會矣
余現未就事外侍不知如何要皆視汝耳在粵東文海書
櫃內有些舊選択可揀有紅圍而涴及墊肥者齊出
寄来幾幅不長一函內當可容納矣
旨昔弟九号

竊也。玩澤古之澤字，便能領會矣。

余現未就事，外傳不知如何，要皆訛傳耳。在《粵東文海》書櫃內有些舊超然報，可揀有紅圈而涉及熱河地勢者，剪出寄來。篇幅不長，一函內當可容納矣。六月廿一日 弟九號。

諭漢兒者此月十三發第十二號囬仪接唇萬十號表

筆已寄到數日因日來為遣汝毋囬耶冬衣畋
費功夫故未赐給汝諭帖耳汝毋茜赵大連趁
船（伯照名支方钵）大的須芝游開由連開行看十日內
外可抵家矣　在香港當此問一切情形俟寅到家
便悉 杳表處余將起程寺借貨百元他日收租有敷
餘宜便還之汝旺樓表先將此話告訴他
廣欠款汝可告冠文九公收齊各堂炭金便可先
還一年餘三百兩一筆則遲两三月還他尚可本指芝
港紙二百元及鄉約揭款之息銀還他今港紙服用

FRANCIS WANN

LETTER 7
To Son Fu, etc,

Did you get my No 12 reply sent on 13th this month? I've received your mail No10 a few days ago and haven't got around to writing as I'm busy sorting out mum's winter clothing for her return. Your mum will wait for the ship in Dailin on 24th (Gilliput from Bellman), which will not leave until 27th and should arrive home in about ten days (not stopping in Hong Kong). Everything here will be clear when she's back. I borrowed $100 from cousin Chun when I left, and will return it when we've collected the rent. Have a word with cousin Tsai about this when you see him. As for the debt owed to Han Chi, tell uncle Koonman to pay him in part from the coal money collection, while the remaining 300 taels can be delayed by two to three months. It was originally agreed that we repay $200 plus interest derived from land mortgages. Now that money has been spent, we have to wait for the rents to make it up. Your mum will return to sort out her clothes and will stay for half a month before coming back here, and may need $20 to $30 for the trip. We'll try to fix it, any way.

I heard the markets for mulberries and silkworms are not good (from Lok Chi's mail). It's also too hot and the pond fish have fallen ill. It's unlikely we can collect the rents in full from our ponds. Poor me!

Remind mum to bring phoenix leaf ashes and the grey cheongsam when she comes.

When you read Han Yu's (1) works, it's better to read those with explanatory notes. There's one in the book cabinet from Tung Ngatong. Though it's a reprint, it is the most detailed and accurate. You may read it but don't damage it.

Earlier you said you seemed to understand something when you read Han's "On Poverty". It's similar in structure to "On

散侯租到湊齊此數乃歸還耳、汝毋歸取衣約
信半月復此來屆時或需三十元乃能成行可
設法籌足與之聞今年發賣柴無價又大熱魚塘
多病看來基塘租不易收足奈何
告汝母此來時記得帶梧桐葉灰及灰布長
衫為要
汝讀辭文宜擇有註者讀之本書櫃內有東雅
堂刻本最精詳可取閱勿污損也汝前云讀过
竈文有悟處此文與毛穎傳進學解諷篇同體宜詰
讀之又柳州之鞭賈梓人傳等皆同一類柳集內此
等文尤多均可誦也

七月廿子第十三号

Learning", and "Muwing's Biography", and it's better to read them together. "Binjia and Sunren's Biography" by Liu Zongyuan (2) belong to the same genre. His collections are full of this type of writing, which are good for recital. July 25. No 13

諭復兒等此月十三發弟十二號回得信接否？第十號來稟已寄到數日。因日來為着汝母回取冬衣，略費功夫，故未暇給汝諭帖耳。汝母廿四赴大連趁船（船名芝力鉢伯銘公司所管），大約須廿七始開，由連開行，十日內外可抵家矣（在香港當不停留）。此間一切情形俟渠到家便悉。椿表處余臨起程時尚借其百元，他日收租有敷餘，宜便還之。汝晤椿表先將此話告訴他可也。漢馳處欠款，汝可告冠文九公收齊各堂炭金便可先還一筆，餘三百兩一筆，則遲三兩月還他亦可。本指定港紙二百元及鄉約揭欵之息銀湊齊還他。今港紙既用散，俟租到湊齊此數乃歸還耳。汝母歸取衣約住半月，復北來，屆時或需三二十元乃能成行，可設法籌足與之。聞今年蠶桑無價（是樂之來函所言），又大熱，塘魚多病，看來基塘租不易收足。奈何！告汝母，北來時記得帶梧桐葉灰及灰布長衫為要。

　　汝讀韓（愈）[7]文宜擇有註之本，書櫃內有東雅堂刻本。雖覆刻本，然最精詳，可取閱，勿污損也。汝前云讀送窮文有悟處，此文與毛穎傳，進學解兩篇同體，宜並讀之。又柳（宗元）[8]州之鞭賈梓人傳等皆同一類，柳集內此等文尤多，均可誦也。七月廿五日。弟十三號。

---

7 Han Yu (768-824), courtesy name Tuizhi, Tang dynasty historian, poet, and Government official whose works have significantly influenced the development of neo-confucianism.
8 Liu Zongyuan (733-819), writer, politician, poet, and a leading figure in the classical prose movement. One of the eight prose masters of the Tang and Song dynasties.

諭 覆見昨農弟西號回內有諭達見
一帖致伯銘一函均為赴港讀書事也
榮弟一課程表與果兒須貼諸書
柏壁上俾其照表遵行如有一件不
遵即將每月果餌錢罰去仍告汝母
我責務使遵行另一緘致冠文九公
汝出可同觀叩週知多事也
　　龢字 七月三十日第十五號

今年代三 姑母收祖叩時送去啟愛我一言

FRANCIS WANN

LETTER 8

To Son Fu,

I sent out reply No 14 yesterday with a message for Tat and a letter to Pakming. They are all about studying in Hong Kong.

I have just issued a study timetable for Kwo, which should be pasted on the wall above his desk so that he can follow it accordingly. If there is even one item that he doesn't observe, his monthly allowance will go. You should also tell Mum to punish him and make him obey. The other letter is for (your) ninth uncle Koonman and you may also read it to understand everything.

Yi

July 30, No 15

You will have collected rent for your third aunt this year. Did you take it to her immediately? Drop me a line.

諭復兒：昨發弟十四號回，內有諭達兒一帖，致伯銘一函，均為赴港讀書事也。

茲發一課程表與果兒，須貼諸書檯壁上俾其照表遵行。如有一件不遵，即將每月果餌錢罰去，仍告汝母戒責，務使遵行。另一緘致冠文九公，汝亦可取觀，以週知各事也。

毅字。七月三十日 弟十五號。

今年代三姑母收租。即時送去否？覆我一言。

諭復兒廿六號至五月又得汝十四號來
寧知汝於母十七動身北來然計期尚在港
多住數日北來船須廿四五乃開也余前教
函屬要多物並不至遺漏卯保遺漏亦祀
要緊之物耳余因手痛尚未復元未寫
所言貨果兒所間多條暫不能答覆只我
應次費田之函屬辦各事汝須貼好隨時檢出
查核有未辦者宣室告未我記性近又差些
因事務太多之故省汝多單寫來寧帖多未合
體裁汝宜教之果字不似信字間渠憶否 八月廿七號

FRANCIS WANN

LETTER 9

Dear Son Fu,

Sent out No 16 on the 20th, and got No 14 from you the next day about your aunt coming over on 17th. Thought she'd stay in Hong Kong for a few more days. North-bound ships would normally depart on the 24th or 25th. Hope you won't leave out any items I mentioned in my last few letters, but even if you forget occasionally, they're not so important anyway. My hand is still in pain, and thus can't answer your and Kwo's questions now. But you should keep my letters to check if everything I mentioned is done, and let me know if it's not so. My memory is failing me again these days. Perhaps there are too many things to attend to.

Most of your younger brothers' letters are not properly structured. You'd better coach them.

Kwo's handwriting is not as good as Shun's. Shame on him! August 24, No 17

諭復兒：廿發回十六號。翌日又得汝十四號來稟，知汝影母十七動身北來，然計期當在港多住數日。北來船須廿四五乃開也。余前數函囑帶各物想不至遺漏，即偶遺漏亦非要緊之物耳。余因手痛尚未復元，來稟所言暨果兒所問各條暫不能答覆，只我歷次發回之函囑辦各事，汝須貯好，隨時檢出查核，有未辦者宜稟告來。我記性近又差些，因事務太多之故也。汝各弟寫來稟帖多未合體裁，汝宜教之。果字不如信字，問渠愧否！八月廿四十七號。

You asked in your letter which are the best among Han Yu's (1)[9] several hundred articles. You may try to read as much as

---

9 Han Yu 韓愈 (768-824), Tang poet, politician and writer whose works significantly influenced the development of neo-confucianism.

東坡問韓文數百篇以何者為佳汝且如唐宋文醇內
之鈔文畫讀玩艾評諭而檢東雅堂韓集互校看
共注釋 蓋不看注則不知艾文之來歷與作者當時之地位
不讀文醇評諭不能暢通曲暢得艾精理也
蘇溪詩鍾汝嚴軍一聯奇才与黃州集是強湊的用
奇才須達明先帝字樣方是一氣若取黃州集對太极
圓則解改奇才為詩才較妥然不若蘇井檀溪一聯忠
渾成也 殷盤睡好汝所作清露底稿寄來西用別紙
另抄過投卷所作弧露獨清中露上清露肺清角露游
清江數聯尚穩妥
冬月十一日父字
弟芝兒

possible of the works of Tang and Song authors, and take note of their reviews and comments (comments from emperors are usually the most accurate and precise). Then compare their explanatory notes and analysis against Dongyatang's (2)[10]

Notes on the *Collected Works of Han Yu*. If you don't read the notes and comments, you won't know how and why the author wrote what they did, in what capacity, and under what circumstances. And you may not further understand the implications and the message.

You came fourth in the Suxi poetry competition, but your choice of "rare talent" and *Wang Chau Anthology* (3)[11] in your couplet was a bit of a stretch. If you use "rare talent", you would probably need to use terms such as "glorious past emperors" to get a sense of the classics. If you put Wang Chau Anthology against Taijitu (4)[12], it's better to change "rare talent" to "rare poet", but still it wouldn't be as holistic as "Sujing Tanxi" in comparison.

Yesterday Yanpoon sent me the original scripts of your work "Clear Dew", and rewrote them on other paper for submission. Your several couplets such as "gulu duqing", "zhonglu shangqing", "lujin qingjiao", and "luxu qingjiang" were all right.

November 11, No 27

Dad

來稟問韓文數百篇，以何者為佳？汝且將唐宋文醇之韓文盡讀，玩其評語（御批最精切），而檢《東雅堂韓集》互校看其注釋。蓋不看注則不知其文之來歷與作者當時之地位。不讀文醇評語不能旁通曲暢，得其精理也。

---

10 Dongyatang Notes to Collected Works of Changli, included in *The Complete Library in Four Sections*.
11 *Wang Chau Anthology* (黃州集), poetry works by Su Shu 蘇軾 (1037-1101), Song poet, politician, calligrapher, writer, and gastronome.
12 Taijitu 太極圖, by Zhou Dunji 周敦頤 (1017-1073), Song dynasty philosopher, cosmologist, believed to be founder of Neo-confucian cosmology and neo-confucianism

LOYAL TO THE END

　　蘇溪詩鐘，汝殿軍一聯，奇才與黃州集是強湊的。用奇才須達明先帝字樣，方是一典。若取黃州集對太極圖，則改奇才為詩才較妥，然不若蘇井檀溪一聯尚渾成也。

　　殷盤昨將汝所作清露底稿寄來，而用別紙抄過投卷。所作如孤露獨清、中露上清、露筋清角、露緒清江數聯尚穩妥。

　　冬月十一日 父字弟卅七號。

Chen Tzedian's (陳子丹) entry for a writing contest, with remarks from Wen Su

FRANCIS WANN

LETTER 10

To Son Fu,

Letter No 33 was dispatched at the end of last year. Got it? Got your brother's mail 31 on the second day of the year about transferring mortgage from the forty rows to Hau Cheung House for $2,000 and saving on interest. It seems like asking Hau Cheung to pay for our interest. How can we feel comfortable about it? And what could we say if it is challenged? (Everyone knows we get credit from the shops for rituals and monthly expenses) It's proper to pay for our mortgage ourselves.

We still have no clues about your brother's education. Earlier I heard Wainam would teach at Tzedian's[13] and I immediately wrote to ask Dian, hoping to send Shun to HK to study. Now I received his letter saying that Wai declined the offer and he's found someone else, but still urges Shun to go. I am quite undecided, and perhaps will just wait for half a month to think over whether to return home first and make a decision then. If I'm not returning, I'll send Shun to HK to study.

You'd better come to see our relatives and meet your father's friends. I'd then send someone to receive you. If Kwo is left home alone, he might not study, but we need to have someone at home for contacts. He can write all right, but it'll be a worry if nobody supervises him.

You seemed to be letting off steam at the end of your letter. Please don't! You should be hardworking and self-motivating in your youth, and remarks like "wasting our days away" shouldn't be made in front of the elderly. Better not do so in future.

January 3. No 1
DAD

---

13 Chen Tzedian, alias Chan Buchi 陳子丹, 陳步墀 (1870-1934). Merchant, poet, and philanthropist; owner of Kin Tye Lung (乾泰隆).

簡頁

諭淺見等去臘抄裝卅三號囬海撽查吞開歲二日

得汝第卅一號來李所祿四十排揭欵作為厚昌堂

統揭二千元則予以者郤息銀似此加法甚邸自己

應納之息銀推收厚昌堂代納投心何安且如未出

數第一役人詰問因何要揭二千 塞祭及每月米銀均賬
於各房人所共知

岀恐吾聲以對仍是自揭自納方可今年汝許弟澄

師讀書之事殊無善法初閱緯南就子丹之西席

即丕諭子丹頗著必信赴港附學若撽丹未囬須不

就聘已政延別佢仍殷こ逐信覓往學但余心郎躊躇

姑俟半月後決定仮里与居乃定計出示孩然後

遣信赴港就学汝宜来此者親藉以拜識诸位

父執屈時當遣人擕汝卜果一人在家未免荒廢

学業甚不便一人時通音訊点不可伊尚能執筆

寫字唯無人管束不愿耳汝来学未數語勿作

牢騷之態是大不可少年努力自勵是應當的唯謹

跪老大華譚不庅在老人前說後宜戒之

正月初三第一号

父字

諭復兒等：去臘抄發卅三號回。得接奉否？開歲二日得汝弟卅一號來稟所稱，四十排揭款作為厚昌堂統揭二千元，則可以省卻息銀。似此辦法，是將自己應納之息銀推歸厚昌堂代納，於心何安？且將來出數萬一被人詰問因何要揭二千（墓祭及每月米銀均賒於各店，人所共知），亦恐無辭以對，仍是自揭自納方可。

今年汝諸弟從師讀書之事，殊無善法。初聞緯南就子丹之西席，即函詢子丹，欲着必信赴港附學。茲接丹來函謂緯不就聘已改延別位，仍殷殷邀信兒往學。但余心頗躊躇。姑俟半月後，決定歸里與否乃定計。如不歸然後遣信赴港就學。

汝宜來此省親，藉以拜識諸位父執。屆時當遣人接汝，只果一人在家，未免荒廢學業。然不留一人時通音訊亦不可。伊尚略能執筆寫字，唯無人管束可慮耳。

汝來稟末數語忽作牢騷之態，是大不可！少年努力自勵是應當的。唯蹉跎老大等語，不應在老人前說。後宜戒之。

　　正月初三　弟一號。父字。

FRANCIS WANN

LETTER 11

Dear Son Fu, etc.

I received your brother's letter No 8 on the 5th of this month and replied at once. It should arrive on the 11th. I'm longing for your letters every day. Today I got letter No 9 from your brother which said Mum's almost recovered, and I felt relieved. It doesn't seem to be the pain in the palm, and it's similar to the pain in my hand two months ago. It began with a sore on the back of the hand and looked as if it was about to burst (but it didn't and now it swells up like a longan seed between the index and middle fingers covering the muscle), and in one or two days it turned red and swelled right up to the vein in my arm, causing intense pain. The Japanese doctor said it was periostitis, and it would burst with pus and develop into an abscess. Later I took his medicine and ointment and cured it, but then the same symptoms appeared on my right hand. It was treated in the same way and seems okay now. It's actually like the foot pain in the past. Are Mum's symptoms similar? The doctors say it's arthritis. According to Hung Fan (Huangdi Neijing)[14], it's probably that the wind inside the body hasn't been cleared and this affects circulation. Well, there must be some truth in it. The village physicians mistook it as ordinary sores. How wrong they were!

I'll pay for the ancestral rituals first if Sixth Auntie hasn't any plans, and anyway we mustn't haggle about cost for matters such as this. The contract with Sunkei has been handed over to Siusung. Did Sixth Auntie say anything? Will need to ask him if the contract is mortgaged and interest will go to charity box, as it may not be appropriate for other purposes. It was agreed that the rent of the field for Juilong Barrier be reduced to $120.

---

14 The most authoritative book of medicine in ancient China, possibly compiled by scholars between the Warring Period (475 BC-221 BC) and Han dynasty (206-220)

諭復兒芸此月初五日得汝萬八號來掌曾即答
卷十一號望穿到矢日之際望來訊今日報得汝萬
九号掌知汝毋已愈八九心乃釋然看來此症並非
手心疔与我前月所患手痛相似初左手背腫起
如薔薇要穿的樣子後辛未穿至今禹隆起如龍眼核
一兩日間紅腫及膺之脈門上其痛非常東洋醫
生說此骨膜炎症不治必會流膿成瘡後服女藥
水內外並治粗愈然左手既愈右手隨發一如左手此

年 月 日

此病醫治今已無甚史狀強為往年之足痛也不知

汝母病狀是否為此醫者云此為痺風病洪範云風

淫末疾想未是不錯的鄉間醫誤看作瘡疗大錯了

公家拜忌名費为六嬸無預備可由我先墊此間祭

先不可互相推諉也新基契已交小宗六嬸有另異

言且須問小宗是否拟与作善堂公相若拿去揭銀

作别用兩不交箱則不必聚隆基塋租曾允讓佃

減到一百廿元之數汝查大信言朦收過若干合凡

今數能持一萬廿元否海心沙減去廿元六号西边月
因此圍田太舊鼠耗太多也唯博樂棠基宜託冠文
九公催左祥往概追收過了七月無棄可採則租不
可得矣汝兄弟每日功課照來單所列必合但達
果均懶寫字此是最吃虧的事以後多人每星期宜
一畫來此現世界上有長進步晚間無事丁請九公
教汝芸珠算達克无宜用心習之明年便去做生
意也此次查字雖腕䏭平但仍欠潤紫毫筆須時之
滿川水也 七月十三第十二号
來字邊求之邊字誤,宜作要乃合

Please check the book and see how much was received from him last year and whether the total amount of $120 is met with this year's contribution. Reducing $20 for Hoisumsa is okay as the fenced paddy is too old, and there are too many rats. However, we should ask Uncle Koonman to get Jorcheung to recover the rents from Pokchun Mulberry Foundation. There will be no mulberries for picking after July, and no rents to collect at all.

Your brothers seem to have complied with their daily homework requirements. But both Tat and Kwo are lazy in calligraphy practice, and that will only do themselves harm. From now on they must send a letter every week so I can check their progress. In the evening, they can learn abacus from their ninth uncle. Tat, you must pay more attention as you'll start doing business next year.

From your writing, it seems you couldn't articulate your wrist well as it's still not supple and smooth enough. Purple brushes need to be soaked quite often.

July 13. No. 12

The word 邀 in your letter (request) was misused. It should be 要.

諭復兒等：此月初五日得汝弟八號來稟當即答發，十一號想寄到矣。日日盼望來訊，今日將得汝弟九號稟知汝母病已癒八九，心乃釋然。看來此症並非手心疔，與或前月所患手痛相似。初在手背腫起如蓄膿要穿的樣子（後卒未穿至今尚隆起如龍眼核大，在食指壯指之間，蓋筋頭也），一兩日間紅腫及臂之脈門上，其痛非常。東洋醫生說此骨膜炎症，不治亦會流膿成瘡。後服其藥水，內外兼治，將愈。然左手既愈右手隨發一如左手，亦如法醫治今已無恙。其狀殆為往年之足痛也。不知汝母病狀是否如此？醫者云此為痛風病。洪範云，風淫末疾，想來是不錯的。鄉間醫誤看作瘡痛，大錯了。公家拜忌各費，如六嬸無預備可由我先墊。此關祭先，不可互相推諉也。新基契已交小宋，六嬸有無異言？且須問小宋是否按與作善堂公箱。若拿去揭銀作別用而不交箱，則不可也。聚隆基墾租曾允該佃減到一百廿元之數。汝查大簿，去臘收過若干合以今數能符一百廿元否？海心沙減去廿元亦無可如何。因此圍田太舊，鼠耗太多也。唯博粲桑基，宜託冠文九公催左祥往欖追收。過了七月，無桑可採，則租不可得矣！

汝兄弟每日功課照來稟所列亦合，但達果均懶寫字。此是最吃虧的事。以後各人每星期寫一稟來以覘汝等之有無進步。晚間無事，可請九公教汝等珠算，達兒尤宜用心習之，明年便去做生意也。

此次來稟，字雖腕較平，但仍欠潤。紫毫筆須時時涵以水也。

七月十三日 弟十二號

來稟邀求之，邀字誤，宜作要乃合。

FRANCIS WANN

LETTER 12

Dear Son Fu, etc

No 4 was sent on the 4th. Did you get it? I now plan to move to Shenyang before the 20th, then I will send someone to fetch you. Money collected in day time should first be remitted to Cheung Pakching in town and redirected to Chaknam. You may let Chak know and he'll ask Cheung to keep the letter. Of this $400, keep $200 for the household, the remaining $200 should be changed into HK currency for ship tickets. Originally I intended to bring both Kwo and Shun here, but on second thoughts I'd rather only bring Shun as I'll probably be back by August. You'll stay here and Shun will come with me as he's qualified for a half-price child fare. If Kwo also comes, the trip will cost more than a hundred dollars extra, and all for only a few months. There's no logic to it! Ah Tat is fifteen, and Kwo is also fourteen. Can't say they are too small. They need to be serious about their future, and I can't always be here to teach them. You may use my words to explain it to them. I hope they won't go out and hang around with the pimps. At home they should practice calligraphy, do reading and chores. As for his studies, I can fix it when I return.

Remember to bring the Guangxu Imperial Instructions with the box (pick out the draft contract and keep it safe). Later you will meet Uncle Pakming in Hong Kong. Bring the five paintings and calligraphy works here, the ones I kept earlier. It's easy to find Japanese buyers, and if sold, I will repay $1,000 to Cen[15]. I will need a suitcase for the paintings. We got some medium-sized ones at home, and the one with a red inside label "RESIDENCE OF HANLIN WEN" would be best. Maybe some repair is needed.

12th No 5

---

15 Cen Guangyue 岑光樾 (1876-1960), Jinshi (1904)

諭復兒苏祖及第四号回擦到否現擦於世三十前遷居瀋陽到瀋後乃遣人擦汕日間收欵先滙回省約四百元揚巷和亭張伯清特擇南汝可先知會擇丞知伯清妣姚妣四百元俻二百作家用飯二百換廣港幣作船須票之费余和擦帶達信同来細思只帶信一人而矣因余八月前必回家俻汕在此信則隨余回以攵小孩船車票均照半價算不省费如若多果一人則来往多费百餘元前後不過敎月矣誉諸兒逹今年十五果六十四歲不為辭須要認真做

人為父並能幸‧督責汕可好此言解釋与二人陪但
朋勿出街与無賴子為伍在家勿事嬉戲習字温書萬
涉家務玉於學業須俟余回乃有辦法現尚復不到也
來此要緊帶光緒朝聖訓連箱裝來　箱內有契據記
好來遇港謁伯銘世伯好余前貼下之书画共五件帶　檢起放妥處
來此廣夏日本人易出售‧得以之還本一千元也要帶
字畫便須預備帶一皮箱來家中有中羊皮箱之高貼
有太史第温紅紙條者最合式或須略修理耳
　　　　　　　　　　　　十二日第五号
年　月　日　　　　　　　父字

影西幸爱史毋老病恐有不測暫伊十元亦也汕暫行並告知汕母照行为要

LOYAL TO THE END

Dad

Yingsai's often worried about her Mum's illness. Should anything happen, give her $10, and tell Mum to heed my words when you leave tomorrow.

諭復兒等：初四發弟四號回，接到否？現擬於二十前遷厲瀋陽。到瀋陽後乃遣人接汝。日間收款先滙回省（約四百元廣毫），揚巷和亨張伯清轉擇南。汝可先知會擇，函知伯清照收也。此四百元留二百作家用，餘二百換港幣作購船票之費。余初擬帶果信同來，細思只帶信一人可矣。因余八月前必回家，留汝在此，信則隨余回，以其小孩船車票均照半價算，可省費也。若多果一人，則來往多費百餘元，前後不過數月，正無謂也！達今年十五歲，果亦十四，齒不為稺，須要認真做人，為父豈能常常督責。汝可將此言解釋與二人聽。但期勿出街與無賴子為伍。在家勿事嬉戲，習字溫書兼涉家務。至於學業須俟余回乃有辦法，現尚談不到也。來時要緊帶《光緒朝聖訓》連箱裝來（箱內有契稿，記拾起放妥處）。將來過港謁伯銘世伯，將余前貯下之書畫共五件帶來此處，覓日本人易出售，售得以之還岑 (1) 一千元也。要帶字畫，便須預備帶一皮箱來。家中有中等皮箱，箱內貼有「太史第溫」紅字條者最合式，或須略修理耳。

十二月弟五號 父字。

影西常憂其母老病，倘有不測，幫伊十元可也。汝臨行並告之汝母照行為要。

FRANCIS WANN

LETTER 13

To Son Fu, etc.

No 3 reply was dispatched on January 22. Got it yet?

Your letter No 5 arrived yesterday. Mortgaging the eight *mu* of Sheungka seems to coincide with what I suggested in letter No 3. As for what Koonman said about the donation boxes, I'll write you another note, and you may take it to show him. I am now appointed director of a cultural society, and will soon move to Shenyang (Fengtian). Once settled, I'll send Pangsun back to collect you both and leave Tat at home as he's more interested in odd jobs and not studies. Anyway, you'll only come for a few months, and I'll send you back in July. (August is my late mother's birthday anniversary) But how can we find the money for household and worshipping rituals for these few months? Can't use the port money anyway. I'll send a remittance for travel and household expenses (will be sent to Chaklam's shop. May alert him first.

    Dad

    February 4. No 4

    … and before you get my letter of moving, letters should still be sent to Kam Shing Apartment.

諭復兒等：正月廿二發弟三號回。得奉否？卅五號來稟昨已寄到。以上卡八畝作按，與余弟三號函中所言辦法正合。至冠文來函所說各箱款事，余另書一紙與汝，汝可持往示之。余現定主任一文化會之事，不日遷厲瀋陽（即奉天省城）。遷定後，即著彭新回接汝兄弟來大約拜山後可赴程矣。留達在家，以彼性不近讀書而好管雜務也。汝來亦不過數月，七月必遣汝回（八月余太夫人冥壽也）。但此數月家用並拜山祭祠等費，何從出？埠箱既不可挪，余當滙款回以作川資及家用耳（匯款即照擇南所開之鋪滙回。可先知會渠也）。

諭復兒等正月廿二發第三號函以來居卅五號來奉
昨已寄到以上卡八欵作據与余第三号函中所言办
法正合玉冠文來函所說各箱欵事余另壹紙与汝之
可執往示之 余現定任一文化會之事不日遷居潘
陽遷定後即著彭新囬攜汝兄弟來省達在家以後
性不近讀書好管雜務也汝來去不過數月七月必遣囬
囬自余去夫人但此數月家用益拜山祭祠芋費何從出毕
冥壽也 滙欵即旺擇南雨闹之鋪滙囬可先知會集也
箱阮不可挪余當滙欵囬以作卅賢及家用耳 父字二月四
年　月　　日 未接余還席信卽前來省仍舊寄金城别墅交爱
号第四

第頁

達吾兒知之 前十三號來稟寄到已久汝兄昨
日寄汝一緘諒接否 將來六孃回家肯帶達
往省讀西文汝達便可隨去但須認真學習
勿再嬉遊益常寄稟未為要汝果在家務要
常寄稟來勿過簡藉以覘汝之文筆通順且
欲多知家事也寄稟來之小楷字毫無進步尚
不及汝弟信之楷書深為汝恥之 外一紙送
吾冠文九公勿悮為要 四月十五第十三號 父諭

父字 二月初四 弟四號。未接余遷厲信以前，來稟仍舊寄金城別墅，又及。

To my sons Da & Guo,

Your letter No 12 arrived long ago. Your brother sent you one yesterday. Have you got it? In future when Sixth Aunt returns, if she agrees to take Tat to town to learn English, you can go with her. But, Tat, you must be serious about your studies and not play around. You must also send me letters more often. Kwo, you are home and should also write to me more, and don't be too short so that I can see if your writing is smooth and coherent, and know more about things at home.

There's no improvement in the small formal characters you sent me, and can't be matched with the calligraphy of your younger brother Shun. I feel shame for you!

The note outside is for Ninth Uncle Koonman. Do not delay.

April 15. No 13

Dad

達果兩兒知之：前十二號來稟寄到已久。汝兄昨日寄汝一緘得接否？將來六嬸回家肯帶達往省讀西文，汝達便可隨去，但須認真學習，勿再嬉遊，並常寄稟來為要。汝果在家亦要常寄稟來，勿過詞簡，藉以覘汝之文筆通順，且欲多知家事也。

寄來之小楷字毫無進步，尚不及汝弟必信之楷書，深為汝恥之。外一紙送去冠文九公，勿誤為要。四月十五 弟十三號 父諭。

FRANCIS WANN

LETTER 14

To Da & Guo,

I sent Pangsun back on February 29 to collect your elder brother and Shun, your younger brother. Maybe they'd left by the time this mail arrived. No 7 from your elder brother arrived yesterday, and from now on you'll continue from his number for your weekly dispatch. Even if there's nothing urgent, a formal greeting is still necessary, and also I can then know if things are all right at home.

You both should revise the learned texts and classics from the Tang and Song Dynasties daily. Do calligraphy according to a plan. Enclose one page of small formal characters in your weekly letter so I can check your progress. Servant Pang forgot to bring you some brushes this time. You may ask your elder brother for some in the small size if he hasn't left. I think you still have some of the brushes I sent last year. Remind your brother to bring the Imperial Instructions of Emperor Guangxu.

March 3. No 9

… and future correspondence should be addressed to Wan Pakon c/o New Travel Agent at South Manchurian Route, Fengtian Station, Shiyiwei Lu.

諭達果知之：二月廿九遣彭新回接汝阿哥及汝信弟，計此函寄到或已起程矣。汝哥哥弟七號來稟昨已收到。此後汝兄弟接續阿哥前稟號數，每星期寄一稟來，雖無要事，但請安亦不可缺，亦藉知家中平安也。

汝兄弟每日溫舊所讀之經及唐詩古文，寫字亦須日有程式。每號稟帖來，夾入小楷書一紙，藉以驗功課之有無進步也。

此次彭僕回，忘寄些筆與汝等。如汝哥哥未動身，可問他要些小筆。去年寄回之筆想未用盡耳。又《光緒朝聖訓》一書記得帶來，並向汝哥提及為要。

諭達知之、二月廿九遣彭新回攜汝阿哥及汝信弟
計此函寄到或已起程矣汝哥與第七號來掌昨已
收到此後汝兄弟攜續阿哥前掌鏡數每星期寄
一掌來雖無要事但請安亦不可缺藉知家中平安
也汝兄弟每日溫舊所讀之經及詩古文寫字必須
日有程式或每發掌帖未夾入小楷書一紙藉此以驗功
課之有無進步也此次彭僕回忌寄些筆與汝芳如
汝哥未動可問他要些小筆去年寄回之筆想未用盡耳
又光緒朝聖訓一書記得帶未并向汝哥提及為要二月三日
以後寄函寫南滿路綫奉天驛十一緯路新旅社溫伯英轉交達也又及
　　　年　　月　　日　第九號

三月三日　弟九號。以後寄函寫南滿路綫奉天驛十一緯路新旅社溫伯安當能妥達也。又及。

The Compendium is now with my third brother. When I was twelve, the Minister of Agriculture taught me, but this was actually an unfinished work of Zhu Xi, and its remark about the history of calligraphy wasn't very convincing. Qianlong decided to edit the compendium. When the Complete version appeared, fewer people read the original edition. The remark about methods seems to have come from the pre-Qianlong era.

For the origins of metaphysics, Taoism, and neo-Confucianism, you may read the first chapter of my philosophy lecture notes, but we only have *Concise Notes on Philosophy*, which include the works of the five philosophers in the Song Dynasty. It's quite difficult and you may not understand it, but you may try. I've bought "Record of Recent Thoughts" which may make it easier to understand neo-confucianism. Chan Pakto[16] borrowed it when he was in Hong Kong. It's not possible to get it back now. Whether having moral virtues and making statements are different was well expounded in Zeng Guofan's[17] "Responding to Liu Xiaxian." The first part is about rites, and the second part is about self-enhancement. It's also included in the *Complete Compendium* selected by Wang Xianqian[18] in The *Collections of Four Schools*. You may pick it out and read it.

November 17. No 28.

…綱目家有此書現在三宅處。余十二歲時　司農公曾教余讀此書，然此書實是朱子未成之書，又其書法發明等註多牽強，故乾隆朝　詔編通鑑輯覽一書以補正之，自有《通鑑輯覽》而綱目少人讀

16　Chan Pakto 陳伯陶 (1855-1930), Qing dynasty Tanhua (探花)
17　Zeng Guofan 曾國藩 (1811-1872), late Qing scholar and politician
18　Wang Xianqian 王先謙 (1842-1917), Jinshi during Tongzhi reign (同治)

綱目家有此書現在三宅庵余十二歲時 司農公曾教余讀
此書然此書實是朱子未成之書文史書法發明苦多
章強故乾隆朝 詔編通鑑輯覽一書以補正之自有
通鑑輯覽而綱目少人讀矣然汝言當是乾隆以前
人語也
性理道術之源流油可知余所著哲學講義首篇讀
之便悉理學宗佛家肉吾此書只有性理精義一來肉
輯宗五子所著書甚深奧汝讀之未必解始試讀之余不
有近思錄一書推理學較易解左港時為陳文良已借去余
可取囬之去
立德立言是否分為二事曾文正答劉霞仙書言之甚晰
此書前半言禮後半言立德立言囧家文鈔內有之王選綾吉文辭類纂
內亦有之可檢閱也 或稱答劉孟容書囧人也
十月十七日廿八号

矣。法語所言尚是乾隆以前人語也。性理道術之源流，汝可將余所著《哲學講義》首篇讀之，便悉理學宗傳。家內無此書，只有性理精義一書，內輯宋五子所著，書甚深奧，汝讀之未必解，姑試讀之。余本購有《近思錄》一書，於理學功夫較易解，在港時為陳文良公借去，今不可取回矣！

　　立德立言是否分為二事，曾文正有《答劉霞仙》一書，言之甚晰。此書前半言禮，後半言立德立言。《四家文鈔》內有之王《選讀古文辭類纂》內亦有之可檢閱也。（或稱答劉孟容書，同一人也）。十一月十七日 廿八號。

然獨不觀艾上文云非三代兩漢之書不敢觀非聖人之志不敢存此所謂義理也有義理而後能咸文故余前教汝讀韓文須讀文醇盍看艾評語盖韓文一篇之義理而文醇評註能闡之也昔張滙亭和貝曾文正公之為讀王介甫泰州海陵許主簿許君墓誌銘一篇抑揚抗墜聲之啟俗無不中節文字精神竟能盡出滙亭言下頓悟不待請說而明此推滙亭造詣之深故能悟此令此文載古文辭類纂中汝試撿出讀之看能有領

年　月　日

FRANCIS WANN

LETTER 15

… just only missed the early parts! "Dare not to read books not from the three dynasties and the two Hans, or study the thoughts not from the masters" — that is what we mean by accumulating our knowledge which is basic to our arguments. That is why I said when you read Han's works, you must read the critiques and reviews, as every piece has its theory, and reading the reviews can help clarify it. In the past when Zhang Lianting first met Zeng Guofan, Zeng read Wang Anshi's Obituary of Hui, (chief clerk of Hai Lang District, Tai Province). His intonation and eloquence enhanced the spirit of the piece, and Lian instantly understood without any explanation. That is due to his literary attainments. This piece is included in the *Collection of Classical Works*. You may pick it out and see if you can understand. This part has something to do with continuity, so I just mention it in passing.

Ouyang Xiu's work is easy to understand while Han's is incomprehensible. It's all right that you like Qu. You can change to Han later. Indeed, the principle is the same. As for styles of arguments, you need not bother at this stage.

Master Zeng is brilliant in all areas — philosophy, literature, and science, but hasn't written any books. That questionnaire on the booklist only covers classical writers, but it's not meant to be a grading system.

Kwo and Shun haven't written to me for a long time. How lazy! Do they still have me in their hearts?

We need not return the port collection box next spring. If the family is short of cash, take it as a temporary measure.

December 17

No 1

第頁

會否此一段故事与行氣之説有關故順及之
歐文易解韓文難領會汝喜讀歐文亦佳亦未由
歐而入韓同儔共貫耳至於陰柔陽剛之説汝尚
未了解且不必分別也
曾文正公於經学小学理学無不精通豈無著書
書目問答只列於古文家內非有意抑揚也
果信久無寄来懶惰為此女学中豈尚知有我耶
埠箱明妻不交於家用不敷而內之韓柳也
臘月十七日
父字

……然獨不觀其上文云:"非三代兩漢之書不敢觀,非聖人之志不敢存"。此所謂積義理也。有義理而後能成文。故余前教汝讀韓文,須讀文醇,兼看其評語。蓋韓文一篇有一篇之義理,而文醇評語,能推闡之也。昔張濂亭(裕釗)初見曾文正公,公為讀王介甫[19]《泰州海陵縣主簿許君墓誌銘》一篇,抑揚抗墜,聲之欷歔,無不中節。文字精神意態盡出。濂亭言下頓悟,不待講說而明。此惟濂亭造詣已深,故能悟此。今此文載《古文辭類纂》中,汝試檢出讀之,看能有領會否。此一段故事與行氣之說有關,故順及之。歐[20]文易解,韓[21]文難領會。汝喜讀歐文亦佳,將來由歐而入韓,同條共貫耳。至於陰柔剛陽之說,汝尚未了解,且不必分別也。

曾文正公於經學、小學、理學,無不博通,然無著書,故書目問答只列於古文家內,非有意抑揚也。

果信久無稟來,懶惰如此,心中豈尚知有我耶!埠箱明春不交,如家用不敷,可向之暫挪也。

臘月十七日

卅一號。

19　Wang Anshi 王安石 (1021-1086), Song dynasty poet and politician.
20　Ouyang Xiu 歐陽修 (1007-1072), Song dynasty historian and poet
21　Han Yu 韓愈 (768 -824), Tang historian and poet

柳文之招得西山宴遊記与黃溪記汝既讀之有領悟會而更以久遊記讀之柳文所遊記凡草一也余少時作字祖席記今載於卿志建置略金紫序許序下趙虜即襲遊黃溪記之調西建虜之議賞未盡也旬即脫胎西山記之兩未拔知西山之怪特自脫胎而出當此虜薦或難於撰文之人因以此文出會作周展居詠閱余文第一遂決定刊之題目字逐字洗鍊何讀之可悟作文宜切空題目也又柳文之文法最妙者除宴遊西山記外尚有愚溪詩序於文多有體汝謂讀柳文一篇勝讀昌黎之書啓數十篇則不知文體之名稱也汝亦喜種讀之藥喜亭滕王閣諸記耳又記文亦有用韻者韓文之汴州東西水門記是也汝試檢讀之臘月廿九弟卅三号

FRANCIS WANN

LETTER 16

If you get the feel of "Finally a Trip to the Western Mountains" and "Yellow Stream" by Liu Zongyuan (1), you might as well read all other travelogues. Liu is at his best in travels. When I was young, I wrote one for the plaque at our ancestral temple now included in Longshan Xiang(2) in various temples under Jinzifeng, and I began by imitating the tone of Yellow Stream without suggesting anything about the construction. Next it went flashing with the phrase "... and still haven't realized the Western Mountains' weird uniqueness". When the temple was completed but the writer couldn't be traced, they used the same title for a contest and asked Zhou from the Ministry of Agriculture to judge. My piece came first and got printed.

Liu's(1) best pieces, apart from "The Western Mountains", may also include "Preface to the Foolish Stream" in which the title was thoroughly explored, word for word. Read it and you'll understand why it's important to set your topic right. You said reading one piece of Liu's work is better than ten pieces of correspondence from Han Yu. That's because you don't know there are different styles, and you probably haven't come across Han's reportage style like "Yin Hei Booth" or "Preface to The Duke of Teng Lodge". And there are also rhymed pieces in narratives, like "The East and West Watergate of Bian Province", also by Han Yu. Try to pick it out and read it.

柳²²文之《始得西山宴遊記》與遊黃溪記，汝既讀之有領會，可更將各遊記讀之。柳文中以遊記為弟一也。余少時作字祖廟碑記（今載於鄉志²³建置略金紫峰諸廟下），起處即襲《遊黃溪記》

---

22 Liu Zongyuan (773-819),Tang dynasty poet, writer, and politician.
23 Longshan Xiang (龍山鄉志), Wen Su (1919), Reprint 1992 (Jiansu Ancient Book Publishing House), Reprint 2018 (Wen Su Edition)

之調而建廟之議尚未起也。句即從西山記之而未始知西山之怪特句脫胎而出。當此廟落成，難覓撰文之人。因以此題出會課，周辰臣評閱余文第一，遂決定刊之。

　　柳文之文法最好者，除宴遊西山記外，尚有《愚溪詩序》於題目字逐字洗發。讀之可悟作文宜切定題目也，又文各有體，汝謂讀柳文一篇，勝讀昌黎之書啟數十篇，則不知文體之各別也。汝未讀韓文之《燕喜亭》、《滕王閣》諸記耳！又記文亦有用韻者，韓文之《汴州東西水門記》是也。汝試檢讀之。臘月卄九　弟卅三號。

FRANCIS WANN

LETTER 17

DAILY TIMETABLE FOR BIGUO
MORNING
Before 9:00 a.m. Read *Book of Historical Records*. After reciting, do dictation. Study thirty lines of *Historical Records*, more if lines are short. Read until all words are clear, and can roughly recite.

NOON
Calligraphy. Limited to 1,000 words. Write in squares for large characters, and do copies of various pages in "The Drunken Man's Booth", or do classical poetry from *Collected Works*.

AFTERNOON
Read Historical Records.

AFTER LIGHTS ON
Read classical poetry. Revise classical works (odd days for poetry, even days for writings. Read until you can recite.

Write a long letter every seven days to replace writing. Minimum 300 words. Ask me in writing anything in the book you don't understand. Words in proper formal characters.

必果每日課程上午
九點鐘前讀史記。背誦畢，默書，教授史記約三十行。短行多則多授。讀識字，約略上口乃輟

中午
習字，以千字為限。大字寫方格，小字臨影本《醉翁亭》記諸片，或鈔文選諸古詩

必果每日課程

上午　九點鐘前讀史記背誦畢默書、教授史記約三十行、短行多則多授　讀識字約略上口乃輟

中午　習字以十字為限、大字寫方格小字臨影本

午後　讀史記、醉翁亭記諸片或鈔文選諸古詩、

上燈後　讀古詩、溫古文、隔日讀詩、柔日溫文、要以能背誦為限

每七日寫一長函寄來以代作文、至少亦須三百字

將所讀之書有疑難者寫來問我、字要端楷

> 来名書目皆是凡紙版同樣者當有數種皆加業叢也
> 也保康送舟車費不宜受 此即祝金愛相余因来未愛返祝金 汝可送回澤馳
> 婉達我意殷盤来孟称蒙曾旬其作囲爐之局朋好
> 酒食来往我不禁汝但不宜飲酒汝體热常手痛鼻衂
> 極不宜酒肴殷盤中年已戒酒忠玉為隆戒也以有
> 正致張老師為我玻後 墓誌文未成出明年安碑未
> 審合今居但前人墓誌文不畫立諸墓只要作者文集
> 中刻有此文便得澤三前輩之母女墓誌石現藏女家也
>
> 年　月　　日
>
> 旅社之旅字未有寫作旅者宜政之 余近
> 遷居頭道溝室町金城外墅下次書来可照
> 此寫や

LOYAL TO THE END

午後讀史記

上燈後
讀古詩，溫古文（剛日讀詩柔日溫文，要以能背誦為限）每七日寫一長函寄來，以代作文。至少亦須三百字。將所讀之書有疑難者寫來問我，字要端楷。

⋯ All the books on the list are paperback editions. There are several similar ones from Kai Yip Books. The travel allowance from Pohong shouldn't be accepted.

(It's like emoluments in disguise; I've never taken any). You may return it to Honchi, stating my point tactfully. Yanpoon's letter mentioned you had asked him to stay for meals. I won't disallow social gatherings among friends, but you must not drink. You're heat-based and have frequent toothaches and nosebleeds. Alcohol is definitely not for you. Just look at Yanpoon's drinking problems in middle age and you'd better stay away from it.

If there is any letter for teacher Mr Cheung, reply on my behalf. The obituary is not ready yet, and I have no idea if it will be the right season to install the tombstone next year. But in the past, people didn't always install it if it was already inscribed in the author's works. The tombstone of Uncle Hansan's (1) mother is now kept at home.

*The word [旅] in 旅社 shouldn't be written as ___. Better correct it. I've recently moved to Toudao Hall at Kinjo Hostel. Use this address next time you write.

⋯⋯來各書目皆是凡紙版。同樣者尚有數種，皆嘉業叢書也。保康送舟車費不宜受（此即袍金變相，余向來未受過袍金）。汝可送回漢馳，婉達我意。殷盤來函稱曾留其作圍爐之局。朋好酒食來往，我不禁汝，但不宜飲酒。汝體熱，常牙痛鼻衄，極不宜酒。看殷盤中年已成酒患，可為戒也。如有函致張老師，為我致候。墓誌文未成出，明年安碑未審合令否？但前人墓誌文不盡立諸墓，只要作者文集中刻有此文便得。漢三[24]前輩之母，其墓誌石現藏其家也。

（旅社之旅字未有寫作＿＿者，宜改之。余近遷居頭道講室町金城別墅，下次書來可照此寫也）

24　Zhang Xuehua 張學華 (alias Hansan 漢三, 1863- 1951), Qing Hanlin, Jinshi in 1890 (Guangxu)

諭澤兒 前月廿九發十六號 計必接十五號未

肇北初五日到矣 汝母初八抵此 無他事

備悉 恰手痛大發 故遲未作書 今

稍漸愈 又穀民師屢過可代我致

吾手痛如此 不知能作墓誌否 祛

廿日製 用我名撰且校切實也

九月十四第十九號

FRANCIS WANN

LETTER 18

To Son Fu,

No 18 was dispatched on the 29th of the month before last. I guess your letter No 15 should arrive on the 5th. Your auntie will arrive here on the 8th. Everything's now ready. However my hand was suddenly in severe pain, so I couldn't reply earlier. It seems to have subsided now. As for Master Kukman, you can send regards on my behalf.

With my hand so painful, I doubt very much if I can write the obituary. I think it would be more practical if I compose it and they do it themselves.

諭復兒：前月廿九發十八號，計得接十五號來稟於初五日到矣。汝影母初八抵此，各事備悉，恰手痛大發，故遲未作書。今始漸愈矣。縠民師處，汝可代我致意。

手痛如此，不知能作墓誌否？請其自製，用我名撰且較切實也。九月十四 弟十九號。

Got the three pieces you sent, which include "Going up the mountain on the 9th". It's clear with a natural flow, and made reference to classics. It must be the result of reading Han poetry. The other two do not develop the arguments well. For such argumentative types, you must have plenty of ideas, then your writing will not sound empty or too general. You're still not well-versed with the *Four Books*. How could you attempt such questions?

You asked earlier if there's a way to make writings shine. Well, good writing does not depend on the choice of words or phrases. For example, Yinyi didn't take anything for himself. The question actually says only a man with an admirable character is capable of holding an important position. Here was someone

寄來文三篇肉九日金峰登高記通體明暢具徵
澤古之功此近來讀漢賦之效也餘二篇未能圍䝶
題蘊此苦理題須胸中積理多下筆乃不膚泛汝
拈四子書全未領會如何能作此等題目汝前問作
文精采之法精采不在字句如伊尹一句不取
讀題真意左有操守人方能營重位一諾畫之
矣惟今日一分不取人之信之如放桐攝政而人不
疑 此彤亭林日知錄 果能造此處發揮透闢便來精
采不筆 也此原作以精一立論便求
深反臨凡文不切題便說之膚廓便不精采矣

who is so honest that everybody trusts him, and later when he was asked to be the regent, nobody objected. (from Gu Tinglin's argument)[25].

If you can elaborate your own views with substance from here, then your work shines. It doesn't depend on any special words. If the original work comes with one single point, then you'll toss it around and examine it from various perspectives. When the writing is off the topic, it will appear loose and shallow, and definitely will not shine!

寄來文三篇，內九日金峰登高記，通體明暢，具徵澤古之功，此近來讀漢賦之效也。餘二篇未能闡發題蘊。此等理題，須胸中積理多，下筆乃不膚泛。汝於四子書全未領會，如何能作此等題目？汝前問作文精彩之法，精采在意不在字句，如伊尹一介不取，該題真意在有操守人方能當重任一語盡之矣！惟其平日一介不取，人人信之，故放桐攝政而人不疑。（此顧亭林《日之錄》之論）。

果能從此處發揮透闢，便是精采，不在乎字句之新警也。如原作以精一立論，便求深反晦。凡文不切題，便謂之膚廓，便不精采矣。

---

25 Gu Tinglin, alias Gu Yanwu (顧炎武 1613-1682). Chinese philologist, geographer, and famous scholar-official in Qing dynasty. He spent his youth during the Manchu conquest of China in anti-Manchu activities after the Ming dynasty had been overthrown. He never served the Qing dynasty

奉呈蒙有致張老師一函可加函寄去間者垣郵
件塞礙殊多招不敢亟寄耳設習字無筆
小楷宜用狼毫有便人再還當煩寄波紫
毫太貴不宜粗用若寸楷羊毫寫寸大書（係湖南筆）
最宜省垣有賣可託人買之即鄭高飛之
雙料烏龍水省垣所有唯須壹做（內託崔直夫壹，備五毫一枝）
此等事便中可託張老師也達見已居赴港
甚念果見竟久無空未何覓頑玉此耶汝
近讀修身書降聰訓齊禮曾家訓外皇朝經世文編中學
術門內有法語一類可常讀以自警也
十月壹貳肆號

FRANCIS WANN

LETTER 19

To Son Fu,

Here's a letter for Mr Cheung. You may send it to Fujian with a covering letter. There are often delays in the town's postal services, so I dare not send it from here.

You have no brush for calligraphy. Use *lang hao* for small formal characters. I will buy and send to you if anyone happens to return.

Zi hao is too expensive for daily use. *Cun gaai yang hao* (brush from Hunan) is best for characters of about one inch in size. It's available in town and I may ask someone to buy it. Indeed they also sell Yin Gaofei's Double Dose Oolongshui but only by order (c/o Cui Zhifu at 50¢ each). You may leave it to Mr Cheung for things like this.

Has Tat left for Hong Kong already? Really miss him. Kwo hasn't written a word. Why so stubborn? If you're reading for self-enhancement, apart from Cun Xun Zhai[26] and Zeng's[27] Family Instructions, there is also something like quotable quotes under *Academic Division in Emperor Ming Articles Compilation*.

You may read it regularly as a self-reminder. October 11. No 14

諭復兒：茲有致張老師一函，可加函寄去閩，省垣郵件室礙殊多，故不敢逕寄耳。

汝習字無筆，小楷宜用狼毫。有便人南還當購寄汝。紫毫太貴不宜粗用。若寸楷羊毫（係湖南筆）寫寸大字最宜。省垣有賣，可託人買之。即鄞高飛之《雙料烏龍水》，亦省垣所有，唯須定做（向託崔直夫定做，五毫一枝）。此等事便中可託張老師也。

---

26 Zhang Ying, Jinshi 1660. Qing dynasty.
27 Zeng Guofan (曾國藩 1811-1872). Qing military general.

LOYAL TO THE END

達兒已否赴港？甚念。果兒竟久無稟來，何冥頑至此耶！汝所讀修身書除《聰訓齋語》(1)，曾家訓外，《皇朝經世文編》中學術門內有法語一類，可常讀以自警也。十月十一日 廿四號。

To Ming Pao My Third Brother's Spirit:
Hardworking. Past millions years. Sad and poor Miss you Brother. Here a few months. Life goes on. Brother Wen Su
明浦三兄老夫子靈几
以勤課隕天年傷哉貧也歎別來曾幾月逝者如斯教弟溫肅頓首拜輓

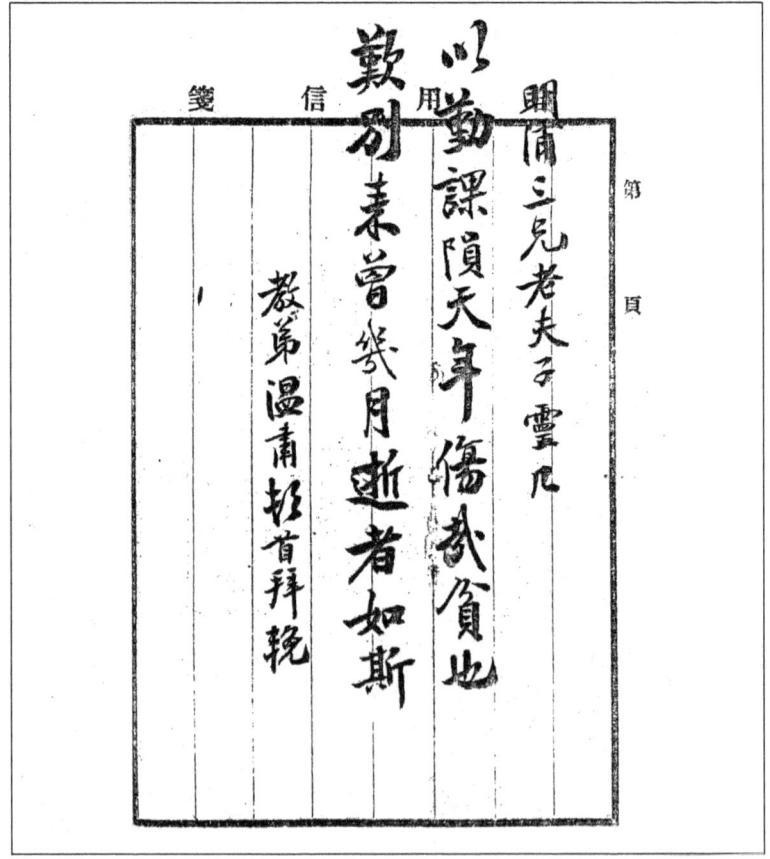

FRANCIS WANN

LETTER 20

Dear Son Fu, etc,

I sent out No 22 on Sept 24. Got it?

Your mail No 19 arrived yesterday, and matters about Mingpo's $20 pledge and draft of the obituary couplet were mentioned earlier. My last letter was a reply to Koonman, and I guess he will do it accordingly. Here's a reply to Sauwo to similar effect, and you may redirect it.

Has your poem "Walking up the Mountain" got listed? What about the one in the fourth place of the poetry contest? Tell me about it. (Who was the judge that day?)

Shun's couplet "Rats are Toothless" (鼠無牙)[28] is neat and well-crafted. It surely is something special! Not only is he way ahead of Tat and Kwo, but you might also have not reached this level when you were ten. You should guide him properly so he won't fall prey to laziness. You're now teaching him the *Book of Poetry*. In the past, you used the original intonation, but now you've changed to Cantonese pronunciation and some confusions are inevitable. Do consult the "Official Edition to the Book of Poetry", examine its phonics and read the explanatory notes, and compare it with others. You may also revise it this way. The poetry edition Tat and Kwo used with punctuation from Master Lupo seems better than others. You may use it to mark the correct intonation and punctuation.

---

28 From Book of Poetry (詩經), Chapter Zhao nan, xing lu: Who says rats are toothless? How can they break my wall? (誰謂鼠無牙? 何以穿我墉?)
"Brother Weihan (Bishen) was then only nine, and I taught him the skills of couplets. One day I challenged him to the task with "Riding on waves, I realise fish have fins (破浪自知魚有刺), he instantly came up with "With holes in the wall, who says rats are toothless?" (穿墉誰謂鼠無牙). Later we were worlds apart, and haven't seen each other for twenty years."
From Bifu's (Wan Chunghan) unpublished manuscripts.
Excerpt from "An initial inquiry into Mr Wan Chunghan's life and posthumous manuscripts" by Kwok Waiting in *Anthology of literary works in Longjiang, 2012*.

諭浚兒蕭九月初五發廿三號回以接昨十九號來稟
昨寄到矣迺明甫奠廿元蓋換聯稿已詳前諭
賢冠文夜函想擱到時必囑辦此若有我守親一
丞必朋前言玉發言汝所作登高詩有吾列名詩
鐘殿軍艾文云何可寫來 每日閱書 信見乘作
風寄書手對極工穩果係自出心裁蓋唯達果
不及即汝十歲時亦未臻此境此宜好之課之勿使
墮懶現汝教伊讀經汝而讀詩經時儀操
正音今改粵音難免訛誤凡每日授經時宜先
看鹽本詩經 四冊有 考其音讀並顧其注釋必自
注者

已溫經之詩也達課前所讀東係蔡蘭公所句讀
致他人考要者即照此點句圈聲西也汝現
讀漢文須將漢書本人列傳先看一遍方能領
會始讀賈山玉言不失明瞭男時情事方知如
言之切舊書櫃內有兩漢策要一書係趙子
昂所書即工兩佳汝閱之萬可得書法之益
王拆父幸隨時升降東漢与西漢較便少渾
穆之氣飲晉六朝食降食異汝但云兩漢文字
与後來特異此證已足外行韓昌黎文起八代
之衰汝試之唐代逆朋八代衰豈可犮哉上月
十月初五

LOYAL TO THE END

Now that you are reading the *Literary Classics*, I'd suggest you read the complete *Biographies of the Book of Han* (漢書) first to get the feel of it. If you read "Words of Jia Shan"[29] (賈山至言) and are not aware of the political situation in that period, how can you feel his sincerity? We have the "Political Summaries of the Hans" in the old cabinet by Zhao Zi'ang (趙子昂)[30]. The printing quality is quite good. Read it and you may benefit more in calligraphy. Judgments on literary works may vary. Those during Han dynasties were less muddy, whereas those in Wei (魏), Jin (晉), and the Six Dynasties were getting increasingly weird. You only said the writings during the two Hans are quite different from those afterwards. It seems like a remark from an outsider. They say Han Yu's (Tang Dynasty) work signaled a revival of literature over eight dynasties. Try counting down from Tang over the eight dynasties and ask yourself since when has literature deteriorated or improved.

October 5

諭復兒等：九月廿四發廿二號回得接否？十九號來稟昨寄到矣。送明甫奠廿元並輓聯稿，已詳前諭，暨冠文覆函，想接到時必照辦也。茲有覆守和一函，亦同前意，可轉去。

汝所作登高詩有無列名？詩鐘殿軍，其文云何？可寫來。（是日閱者為誰）信兒所作《鼠無牙》對[31]，極工穩，果係自出心裁！豈唯達果不及，即汝十歲時亦未臻此境也！宜好好課之，勿使墮入懶惰。現汝教伊詩經，汝前讀詩經時係操正音，今改粵音難免訛誤。每日授經時，宜先看《監本詩經》（四冊有註者），考其音讀兼覽其註釋，亦自己溫經之法也。達果前所讀詩經本係菉甫公所句讀，較他人為妥當，即照此點句圈聲可也。汝現讀漢文須將《漢書》本人列傳先看一遍，方能領會。如讀《賈山

---

29 Jia Shan. West Han dynasty, circa 179 BC
30 Zhao Mengfu (1254-1322), alias Zi'ang. Calligrapher, painter, and scholar of the Yuan dynasty. Descendant of Song dynasty's imperial family through marriage.
31 *Book of Poetry*: "Zhao nan, Xing lu"

至言》[32]，不先明瞭當時情事如何知其言之切？舊書櫃內有《兩漢策要》一書，係趙子昂所書，印工尚佳，汝閱之兼可得書法之益也。至於文章隨時升降，東漢與西漢較便少渾穆之氣。魏晉六朝，愈降愈異。汝但云兩漢文章與後來特異，此語已是外行。韓昌黎文起八代之衰，汝試從唐代逆溯八代看從何代衰起也 ...

　　十月初五。

---

[32] "Jia Shan", from West Han dynasty, c179 BC.

諭復兒芝前旬得汝五月十四來一稟這今未見續來正在覂念中計余前後共發三諭帖回汝接奉後應覆者須一一詳覆為要達稟信名須學作掌帖寄來籍知汝芝文字進步如何前諭已詳及之矣瞬時之汝騰正之龍山矢錄已藏事居鄉兩近日應有冠裳會文題汝有學作否汝近日書法竟走入乾枯一路宜速改回圓秀一路此閱汝福澤尺作字固畫臨仿而筆墨六閒緊要汝芝連調墨只不會宜函請求也

閏月十四　父諭

FRANCIS WANN

LETTER 21

To Son Fu, etc

Got one mail from you dated May 14 a month ago, and nothing else since. I was baffled, as I've sent out altogether three letters. If it's necessary to reply, you should reply to each one in detail.

Tat, Kwo, and Shun all need to learn to write letters and send me so I know their progress in writing. I actually mentioned it in my last mail.

Have you finished rewriting "Writings of Longshan" which I gave you before I left? They should be holding the official writing contest back home these days. Will you try? Recently your calligraphy seems rather dry. It's better to return to the smooth and elegant style soon as it may affect your life in the future.

It is of course important to study the master's calligraphic works when we write, but brush and ink are also important. You don't even know how to prepare your ink. Better pay immediate attention to this.

Leap month 14th Dad

諭復兒等：前旬得汝五月十四來一稟，迄今未見續來，正在懸念中。計余前後共發三諭帖回。汝接奉後應覆者須一一詳覆為要。達果信各須學作稟帖寄來，藉知汝等文字進步如何，前諭已詳及之矣。

臨行時交汝謄正之《龍山文錄》已蕆事否？鄉內近日應有冠裳會文題，汝有學作否？汝近日書法竟走入乾枯一路，宜速改回圓秀一路，此關汝福澤。凡作字固重臨仿，而筆墨亦緊要。汝等連調墨亦不會，宜亟講求也。

閏月十四，父諭。

諭紀見芝前日剛發了一函昨日接汝五月尚未拿到幸課程恰與吾前函同茲可免一慰前所曾交正谷與鄧寅皆函一紙所論看讀寫作缺一不可字之精切汝兄弟當多錄一通細心體認即作為吾之家訓可也爾果如此懶惰不改前非可告汝母將渠閒置祇房中每日除食飯大便乃放出來書籍筆墨一切備具任渠看書寫字有十日功夫心自定矣仍將十日之功課呈我抆來要渠自己寫字不要汝代也來字淋漓字寫作淋灕看擴否求過於供句應作來

FRANCIS WANN

LETTER 22

To Son Fu, etc

Just sent out a letter the day before yesterday. Yesterday I got your letter dated May 14 about the study timetable. I was much relieved as it was similar to my ideas in the last mail. Here's a copy of the Correspondence between Zeng Guofan[33] and Tang Yinjie, which includes an argument that (in learning), "seeing, reading, writing, and composing" are all important and indispensable. It's an excellent article. You brothers should each copy it once, and read carefully. It can also be taken as our family motto.

If Kwo doesn't improve, you can tell Mum to lock him up in his bedroom and only let him out for meals or the toilet. Books and writing materials will be made available. Keep it this way for ten days and he'll be settled. He still has to send me his homework for the ten days, and he must do it himself.

Don't write for him!

> You seem to have mistaken 淋漓 for 淋灘. Got any basis for that?

For an argument on demand exceeding supply, you should argue this from the point of intra-marriage between Qi[34] and Wei[35] States. There's a lot you can elaborate, but the writing fell short of it. Though it claimed to monitor the rise and fall of the tribe, in fact, it was no more than a selfish endeavor of Duke Huan of Qi. General Wukui[36] saved his uncle, and no doubt all for the sake of his consort Wei, though it can be seen during the

---

33 Zeng Guofan, Qing statesman (1811-1872), Marquis Yiyong. Posthumous name Wenzheng.
34 Duke Huan of Qi (?-643 BC), 15th ruler of Qi in the Spring and Autumn Period.
35 Wei Van Cong (?-635 BC), 20th ruler of the Kingdom of Ve in Spring and Autumn Period.
36 Wukui (?-642 BC), first son of Duke Huan of Qi and consort Wei.

篇淫齊衛婚姻之邦立論本極可發揮無如文未解此意須云齊桓此舉明為興滅繼絕實則為私耳與驪姬以甥殺舅與衛姬之陳請無異雖然可見妻秋之初兄弟婚姻之國休戚相切風氣尚古所以秦桓力韶健逆諾阿許穆夫人亦有載馳之賦數十年後奉穆納晉惠則東畫號略周及解梁非賄不行以假婚姻生銅斗之煙至於戰國今日婚媾明日仇讎言合可乎間繼則齊桓此舉雖私而亦空前絕後之事也為此則文勢壯潤波瀾老成不知將來所取多卷有此此立論者耳

early Spring-Autumn Period that this practice had resulted in abuse of power from relatives. Duke Huan I of Song[37] was weak but nonetheless he rebelled against Chuho, and Lady Xu Mu[38] also composed the poem "Zaichi". (Speeding Chariot, from Zuo Zhuan 左傳)

Decades later, Duke Mu of Qin captured Duke Hui of Jin, and expanded eastwards to Guolue, inward to Jialeong. Nothing worked without bribery, and this gradually led to huge financial and marital issues.

As for the Warring States, they could be united by marriage today, but go against each other tomorrow. Who knows?

Duke Huan of Qi was selfish, but what he did was probably unprecedented in human history. An argument like this would be strong, mature, and substantial. I wonder if any papers in future will argue it this way!

諭復兒等：前日剛發了一函回，昨接與汝五月十四來稟讀書課程，恰與吾前函同意可為一慰。茲鈔回曾文正公與鄧寅皆函一紙所論看讀寫作缺一不可，字字精切。汝兄弟當各錄一通，細心體認，即作為吾之家訓可也。

阿果如懶惰不改前非，可告汝母將渠閉置於臥房中。每日除食飯大便乃放出來。書籍筆墨一切備具任渠看書寫字。有十日功夫心自定矣，仍將十日內之功課稟報來。要渠自己寫稟，不要汝代也。來稟淋漓寫作淋漓。有據否？求過於供句，應作篇，從齊衛婚姻之邦立論，本極可發揮。無如文未解此意。

須云齊桓此舉，明為興滅繼絕，實則為私親耳。無虧帥師以甥救舅，其為衛姬之陳請無疑。雖然亦可見春秋之初，兄弟婚姻之國休戚，關切風氣尚古。所以宋桓力弱，尚逆諸河，而許穆夫

---

37 Duke Huan I of Song (?-651 BC). Succeeded by son Duke Xiang of Song in 650 BC.
38 Lady Xu Mu, of 7th Century BC, was princess of the State of Wey, and married to Duke Mu of Xu. First recorded female poet.
    Council minutes (Courtesy of University Archives, HKU)
    Note: Wen Su's name was officially registered as Wan Suk in HKU

人亦有《載馳》之賦。數十年以後，秦穆納晉惠，則東盡虢略，內及解梁，非賄不行。寖假婚姻生銅斗之嫌。至於戰國，今日婚媾，明日仇讐，愈不可問。然則齊桓此舉，雖私而亦空前絕後之事也！如此則文勢壯闊，波瀾老成。不知將來所取各卷有如此立論否耳。

羊毫習大楷紫毫習小楷尖均宜用徐字訣徐者後也緩乃徑貫到鋒尖謂紫毫硬懌不餘鈎捺此走解開紫毫之性紫毫雖長大然所用者只筆鋒一二傈毫耳用到筆肚則毫已壞矣故寫小字仍用狼毫、較爽也

果兌秉字多寫訛字且字帖不能用兩筆函候之誤宜請求措詞之法可讀曾文正家書多讀便會作字且明讀書之門徑矣我少時全讀此書故得力在此汕兄弟宜知之

宣和旨第七號

LOYAL TO THE END

Letter 23

Use *yang hao* for large characters, and *ji hao* for small ones. Anyway, it's better to adopt the 'gradual' approach. Gradual means slow, it also means the ink can reach the tip. Some say *ji hao* is too harsh to do the hook and right downward strokes. That's because they don't understand its quality. Though *ji hao* is longer and big, you only use one or two hairs at the tip. If you're using up to the body, it's already damaged. You still use *lang hao* for small characters. It's easier to handle.

Kwo's letter contains many wrong words. Moreover you cannot address your senior like your peers. It's better to use the proper language. Read more of Zeng Guofan's family letters and you'll learn how to write properly, and also the way of studying. I read it all when I was young, and it helped me a lot. Your brothers must take note of this. June 6. No 7

羊毫習大楷，紫毫習小楷，然均宜用"徐"字訣。徐者緩也，緩乃能力貫到鋒尖。謂紫毫硬強不能鉤捺，此未解紫毫之性。紫毫雖長大，然所用者只筆鋒一二條毫耳。用到筆肚則毫已壞矣。汝寫小字仍用狼毫，毫較爽也。

果兒來稟多訛字，且稟帖不能用朋輩函候之語，宜講求措詞之法。可讀曾文正家書。多讀便會作稟，且明讀書之門徑矣！我少時全讀此書，故得力在此。汝兄弟宜知之。六月初六日弟七號。

... and read from *Sheng Boxi's Anthology*:[39] "The literary works of Mi State is the Best in Northern Yan", four pieces on "Appreciation of Relics in Jiaoshan" and "Tales of Stripes left by Bao Ting", "A visit to The Directorate of Imperial Academy (Guozijian)", and "The Magnificent Ten Drums with Two

---

39 Bao Ting 寶竹坡 (1840-1890). Manchu poet, Jinshi.

及讀盛伯熙集密國文詞冠北燕一首焦山觀寶竹坡留帶
四晉遇國子監巍然十鼓兩司戒一首皆舍當時多少事實
多問多究便添無限興趣矣見讀書貪多務以無序雜
進誠為可憂若能於每日課程分出某書為專科某書為
旁涉積日累月自不難次第功昌矣不云乎毋望其速
咸毋諉於勢利養其根俟其實加其膏而希其光學文然
讀書六然汝試旦之以半年以來汝未嘗未有提過習
東文李豈中撥耶 汝字不是平庸晒憲在結構未臻

囡藝或係求速之故作畫須經過階級乃可求速也近日必信字大進學我愛看上戚相似由共批管的済居鈦擇匯目此矣汝寫說文部首字即以藜永椿之說文解字一字一行存作樣東其篆法頗精嚴此其通挖即附按後家中有此書陳先生所用望此是粵刻無他東也余甚次赴港皆絢伯銘主運無他事也侶文現仍就養中席甚此見婦今日赴港歸寧下月初六第四姊出閤此受文尚間已送衣料及利是矣海外罵六拾下月生日益送稚言也

七月廿四第十三号

Ministers". They all made reference to events of their times. Ask around and do more research and you'll realize the enormous pleasure in it. Once you read too much, you'll find yourself disorganized, which is a pity. In your daily reading, you may pick out subjects of your specialty, and those simply for side interest. Over time, it will not be difficult to see the results. Didn't Changli say this? "Don't expect instant results, don't be tempted by interests. (Like planting) Give nutrient to its root and wait for its fruits, and put in oil (to the lamp) and hope the light will glow…" Writing is like this, and so is reading. You'd better think about it. For almost half a year, you haven't mentioned anything about your study of Japanese. Have you given up?

Your calligraphy is not bad, but the structure isn't smooth enough. Perhaps you're aiming for quick results. There must be a gradual process before any speedy progress.

Bishen has made huge progress in his calligraphy, which much resembles mine. He controls the brush well, and even feels comfortable in whatever he writes.

When you practice the radicals in Shuowen, you may refer to Li Yongchun's[40] Shuowen Jiezi (one word for each column) as his seal characters are quite accurate, and with an index at the end. We have got it at home. I guess Mr Chan also uses this Guangdong block print version, as there are no other versions.

My last two trips to Hong Kong were all arranged by Bakming. There wasn't really anything important. Luiman is now on benefits with quite good allowances. His daughter-in-law will join her family in Hong Kong today, and her fourth elder sister gets married early next month. I've already sent out clothing and laisees. Next month will also be your uncle's birthday, and we'll send him presents.

---

40 Zhang Zhidong, Tang Haoming (1946 -), vice president, Hunan Writers' Association.

LOYAL TO THE END

　　…　及讀《盛伯熙集》:〈密國文詞冠北燕〉一首、〈焦山觀寶竹坡留帶〉四首、〈過國子監〉、〈巍然十鼓〉兩句成一首,皆含當時多少事實,多問及考究便添無限興趣矣。凡讀書貪多務得,無序雜進,誠為可憂。若能於每日課程中分出某書為專科,某書為旁涉,積日累月,自不難次弟程功。昌黎不云乎?「毋望其速成,毋誘於勢利;養其根以竢其實,加其膏而希其光。」[41,][42] 學文然,讀書亦然。汝試思之,只半年以來,汝來稟未有提過習東文事,豈中輟耶?汝字不是平庸,所患在結構未臻圓整,或係求速之故。作書須經過遲緩之階段乃可求速也。近日必信字大進,學我幾有七八成相似。由其執管得法,居然揮灑自如矣。汝寫說文部首字,即以黎永椿之說文解字(一字一行本)作樣本,其篆法頗精嚴也,其通檢即付於後。家中有此書。陳先生所用想亦是粵刻,無他本也。

　　余兩次赴港皆徇伯銘之邀,無他事也。侶文現仍就養中席,所入尚好。兒婦今日赴港歸寗,下月初其第四姊出閣,此間已送衣料及利是矣。汝外舅亦於下月生日並送禮去也。七月廿四。弟十二號。

41　Han Yu, alias Changli 昌黎 (768- 824), Responding to Li Yi.
42　Li Yi, Jinshi in 802, Tang dynasty.

御史中丞 *(Yushi Zhongcheng)*

久不作書因心緒不佳前月為黎親家過去心上殊多感觸因受其臨終囑託照料家事在津多日見昭兒身體尚好外孫点結實共乳須用代乳粉當有喪事時霧阿銀日夕抱著該小孩在樓上總算無用中亦有用耳 雲嬋前日病死了病了五個月花去醫藥錢無數然終無效術者謂我今歲流年不佳玉小也浮破財並傷小口今死一奴一婢當可攤過矣 京中經此一次變局以後不知如何好或不能長住 別須把春遷回可惜兒後兒極聰明能讀書若不跟着我則恐無成耳 餘事容續詳 仲閎近佳
毅 罡芷日

FRANCIS WANN

LETTER 24

I haven't written for a long time as I was not in the mood. My in-law Li (Zhangzhi)[43] passed away a few months ago. I felt so much about it as he pledged me to take care of his family at his bedside. Ah Chiu seems all right here in Tianjin. Grandson is also healthy but has to rely on milk powder. When we were having the funeral, it was fortunate that Ah Ngan the maid took care of the baby upstairs day and night. At least she's useful in a way.

Our maid Wan went after five months of illness. A lot has been spent but still no use. A fortune teller said it's a bad year for me, and at the least I would lose money and my family would get hurt. Now that I've lost a servant and a maid, and it should offset the curse.

After this incident in the Government, I don't know what the future holds. Perhaps I cannot stay here for good, and maybe I have to send my family back home. What a pity as Bifu is so diligent and can study. If he's not with me, I'm afraid he'd end up as nobody. Let's talk when we meet later. Take care.

Yi April 27

久不作書，因心緒不佳。前月為黎親家過去，心上殊多感觸，因受其臨終囑託照料家事。在津多日見昭兒身體尚好，外孫亦結實，只無乳須用代乳粉。當有喪事時，虧阿銀日夕抱着該小孩在樓上，總算無用中亦有用耳。雲婢前日病死，足病了五個月，花去醫藥錢無數，然終無效。術者謂我今歲流年不佳，至小也得破財兼傷小口。今死一奴一婢，當可擋過矣。

京中經此一次變局，以後不知何如，或不能長住，則須把眷遷回。只可惜復兒極聰明能讀書，若不跟着我則恐無成耳。餘事容續詳。即問近佳。

毅 四月廿七日

---

43   Li Zhangzhi 黎湛枝 (1870-1928), Qing dynasty politician.

今晨到津廬英界松壽里六號黎年伯以餞約

三二日內便回京若因

御用橘紅詢及吾家有無存儲余心記不清有存否盡數撿來

如有可檢出封好著人送到南河沿朱宅請其順帶朱師傅來說明朱師傅初十早車必來津也如家中無存另即刻

上用的朱師傅和十早車必來津也

打一電話來騐數撿等也

諭昭兒知之 初八夕

小姓眷閣

FRANCIS WANN

LETTER 25

This morning I went to in-law Uncle Li's residence at 6 Chungsau Lane in Tianjin within the British concession. I will be back in two or three days. They asked if we have any royal-commissioned tangerines. I actually forgot. If we have, pick them all out, seal the pack and ask someone to take them to Master Zhu's residence at South Riverside. Ask him to deliver them here, and mention they're for the royal household.

Master Zhu should arrive in Tianjin on an early train on 10th. Call immediately if we haven't got any in store. Attention Chiuyi. Evening, 8th

今晨到津厲英界松壽里六號黎年伯公館，約三二日便回鄉。茲因御用橘紅詢及吾家有無存儲，余亦記不清有存否，如有可檢出封好，(盡數檢來) 着人送到南河沿朱宅（朱師傅），請其順帶來。說明是上用的。

朱師傅初十早車必來津也。如家中無存，可即刻打一電話來也。諭昭兒知之 初八夕。

諭復兒 前以汝芃先袋來當臨當即示復第六號
信 前十八日
得亨否十九日滙由長春中國銀行滙粤三百圓上海大洋与
朱士高 住鴨旦花八號 由朱換廣毫乃交和亨張伯清約匯
問朱仁便悉
百圓上下 汝見此信後可即函詢朱士高一面託擇南面
知和亨可中 余於昨 廿一日 遷廬濱陽此寄函書南滿路
綫 奉天驛十一緯路新旅社溫伯安收可也 約下月初
一 遣彭新回初十邊可抵鄉 計十五後必有渣華船此
奉屆時同彭新赴港為自当送家耳餘諸前諭 廿三晨七筆
 父字

FRANCIS WANN

LETTER 26

To Sons Fu, Shen,

Got your mail dated 29th and promptly dispatched No 6. Got it? On 19th, I transmitted $300 in Shanghai currency from Changchun Bank of China to Chu Szeko (in town at No 8, Apdanfa. Ask Chu Yan.). Chu will exchange it to Guangzhou currency and hand over around $400 to Cheung Pakching of Wo Hang.

When you receive this letter, write and ask Chu immediately, and at the same time ask Chaklam to write and inform Wo Hang.

I moved to Shengyang yesterday (21st). Your letters may be sent to Wan Pakon, c/o New Travel Agent at Shiyiwei Lu, Fengtien Station, Nam Mun Line, Shenyang. I will send Pangsan back around the first of next month, and should arrive home around the 10th. Northbound Java ships will be available after the 15th, and I'll then come with him to Hong Kong. So there's still time. For the rest, refer to my earlier mail. Yi

February 22. No 7

諭復、信兒：前得汝廿九發來稟帖，當即示復弟六號（二月十八日）得奉否？十九日由長春中國銀行滙粵三百圓（上海大洋）與朱士高（住省鴨蛋花八號，問朱仁便悉）。由朱換廣毫乃交和亨張伯清約四百圓上下。汝見此信後可即函詢朱士高，一面託擇南函知和亨可也。余於昨（廿一日）遷厲瀋陽。如寄函，書南滿路綫奉天驛十一緯路新旅社溫伯安收可也。約下月初一遣彭新回，初十邊可抵鄉。計十五後必有渣華船北來，屆時同彭新赴港，為日尚從容耳！餘詳前諭。

二月廿二日 弟七號。毅字

十月廿四日昭兒自粵回津詳述家中情形
云杜鵑庵東南角有傾欹之處聞之甚為
耿心其餘各地方聞必荒凉殊甚宜催人
來整理單何良一人恐不能舉也
今年祠堂冬祭必須舉行所費無多
設法支持便是吾今年未死而有祠無祭有
定無人理成何景象不是所望於內助矣
寺此順問近好　　諭　十一月初一日

FRANCIS WANN

LETTER 27

October 28

Chiuyi has returned to Tianjin from Guangdong and gave a detailed account of our home. Allegedly the southeastern corner of Cuckoo Hut appeared slanted, and I was deeply worried. Elsewhere the place was reportedly desolate, bleak, and barren. We'd better get some extras to fix it, and Ah Leung can't do it alone (Leung is part of our family, and we should assume he's having meals here with us; must not take him as a servant). This year's winter service at the ancestral hall must be held, and we'll find ways to settle the cost.

I'm lucky to still be alive. We have an ancestral temple but no tributes, and a house which nobody cares about. What kind of state am I in? Now everything depends on my wife.

Best regards,

Yi

November 8

Seal the letter to third brother first before presenting it.

十月卄八日昭兒自粵回津，詳述家中情形，云杜鵑庵東南角有傾欹之患，聞之甚為耽心。其餘各地方聞亦荒涼殊甚，宜僱散工來整理。單阿良一人，恐力不能舉也(良是自己親人，只可當其撈飯餐不能當僕役用也)。今年祠堂冬祭必須舉行。所費多少設法支轉便是。

吾幸未死而有祠無人祭，有宅無人理，成何景象！是所望於內助矣。

專此順問 近好。

毅

頓首 十一月初八日

(三少函封了口方可呈)

香港大學中文學會說詩

古今詩浩如淵海從何說起消奇瀠淡各有偏嗜昔謝太傅讀毛詩取訏謨定命遠猷辰告二句謝征西則
取楊柳依依謝道韞則取棫樸如濆風雲斯以談詩之好尚視乎人身之所處耳今日在座諸君多少年身鄖人亦
經過少年之境少年心理頗能道出少年人大半好雄武風流一派唯鄰佳耶却有癖處於誓武詩妾帶有敵愾同仇
之意者方佳鳳流詩妾嘴得發情此禮者方佳耶如三百篇中鳳之常武江漢六月采芑發揚蹈厲皆爲王事常武
人秩秩德音終不以兒女異鳳雲之氣此聖人所謂思求偶婁周秦行紀渉想何莫不以今人稱誦之謂其合事君之
六章且提出王字斯亦可見古詩人之心理矣至於鳳詩旣佳於小戎之女子雖思念君子至于飢其心曲然一轉念胝帨良
旣如上所云顧亦何常不然哀高郎之無女至十見有娥而賦思求偶婁周秦行紀渉想何莫前古今稻誦之謂其合事君之
道何也史皆曰少年人于詩不淫小雅怨誹前不亂若與梅郎瓢之真如苦哉然猶津津樂道之以見詩
不可無宗旨也專門山本詠寧德公主加入榮昌公主二人身世不同歸叙處寳主分明末復添長平公
然集中布無瑕疵具如梅村司馬怨東樂章掖殿上行束萊行幾篇傑作則如劇焉之無台柱雖妖艶末見得便動人此固
猶著於選題亦見詩之一道焉本思孝方足傳也若前篇詩如閬園山永和宮詞不過起結佳耳餘俠未見怒兔平衍之病娶結構
之精莫如鴛央篇先而先說本事樂安公主後加入榮昌公主二人身世不同歸叙處寳主分明末復添長平公
主一段絶不冗杏且起處由妃后孃妤家折入沁閬公主郎收虚代寒境將先後傳呼喚摊賨妃笑折棚俏囘應起處
不使一滴漏出細細毴透如天衣無縫束萊行之誚美如叚如賓兄弟中間忽挿入宋九青左榻第如邀客要請來即來娑
打發走鄖走樹操縱自如學梅村當于此等處着眼也父梅村雖擅顯然其中有肩意或隱指一事者方有意味若實釓艷
情如琴河感舊四首戲贈十首雖妖冶而不耐觀祝青衫憔悴梻織我紅粉凜零我憶卿此等滄句耶若古意六首則有寫怨
也總之詩中感慨頗多本人玉溪無題多鄖香匯莫不然
便令人低徊欲絶雜怨之武安席上一首倣唐人本事詩四首則有所指耐人探索推之所人玉溪無題多鄖香匯莫不然
情之詩也予欲操詩以言述詩中有人方足傳北詩梅村以賦代逸才遭時鼎革不逸其高節慨慷何伊鬱情兒乎詞而紀事論人是非人
歷故稱詩史後人賊其詩衷其過不偉之於梨雙之發惜其人也然則吾人欲作好詩何不先學作好人乎

150

Footnotes:
1. Liu Yiqing (403-444). "A New Account on the Tales of the World" 世說新語
2. *The Records of the Grand Historian* 史記.
3. Qu Yuan 屈原, (343 BC-278 BC).Warring States Period.
4. Wu Weiye 吳偉業, alias Wu Meicun 吳梅邨 (1609- 1671). Author of "The Story of the Stone" which inspired the creation of "The Red Chamber" by Cao Xueqin.
5. Zhao Yi, (1727-1814). Qing poet and historian

Liang Guangzhao 梁廣照 (1877-1951), Qing scholar, descendant of Liang Jingguo 梁經國 (1761-1837), proprietor of Tian Bao Hong (天寶行), one of the Thirteen Hongs of Canton (廣東十三行) (Courtesy of Leung Kaywing)

香港大學中文學會說詩

古今詩浩如淵海，從何說起？美惡高下無定評，清奇濃淡各有偏嗜。昔謝太傅讀毛詩，取"訏謨定命，遠猷辰告"二句，謝征西則取"楊柳依依"，謝道韞則取"穆如清風"[44]。準斯以談詩之好，尚視乎人身之所處，心之所寄焉耳。

今日在座諸君多少年身。鄙人亦經過少年之境，少年心理頗能道出。以詩境論，少年人大半好雄武風流一派。唯鄙性卻有僻處，於雄武詩要帶有敵愾同仇之意者方佳；風流詩要曉得發情止禮者方佳。即如三百篇中《風》之無衣，《雅》之常武、《江漢》、《六月》、《采芑》、《發揚》、《蹈厲》-皆為王事。《常武》六章且提出王字，斯亦可見古詩人之心理矣。至於風詩，莫佳於《小戎》之女子。雖思念君子至于亂其心曲，然一轉念，厭厭良人，秩秩德音，終不以兒女累風雲之氣。此聖人所舉示詩旨。所謂邇之事父，遠之事君；又曰詩無邪也。今人開口動言風騷，《風》既如上所云，騷亦何常不然？哀高邱之無女，至于見有娀而輒思求偶，與《周秦行紀》[45] 涉想何異？而古今稱誦

44　劉義慶 (403- 444), 世說新語，第二門 (言語)
45　史記 (91 BC).

之，謂其合事君之道，何也？史遷曰"《國風》好色而淫，《小雅》怨誹而不亂，若《離騷》[46]者，可謂兼之。"真知言哉！凡此皆陳言，然猶津津樂道者，以見作詩不可無宗旨也。

少年人于詩既具此好尚，其于近代詩必喜吳梅邨[47]。《甌北詩話》[48] 稱梅邨詩"千嬌百媚，妖艷動人"，可謂善於形容。然集中苟無《臨江參軍》、《鴈門司馬》、《後東皋草學堂》，《殿上行》，《東萊行》幾篇傑作，則如劇場之無台柱，雖妖艷未見得便動人。此固猶善於選題，亦見詩之一道，原本忠孝方足傳也。若篇篇如《圓圓曲》、《永和宮詞》，不過起結佳耳，餘尚未免平衍之病。

要論結構之精，莫如《簫史青門曲》。本詠寧德公主而先說樂安公主，後加入榮昌公主，三人身世不同，鋪敘處賓主分明，末復添長平公主一段，絕不冗沓。且起處由妃后嬪妤家折入沁園公主第，收處借夢境將先後傳呼喚捲簾、貴妃笑折櫻桃倦，回應起處，不使一滴滲漏，其細密處真如天衣無縫。

《東萊行》之詠姜 如農須兄弟，中間忽插入宋九青，左懋第如邀客要請來即來，要打發走即走，極操縱自如，學梅邨當于此等處着眼也。又梅邨雖擅艷體，然其中有寓意或隱指一事者，方有意味。若實寫艷情如《琴河感舊》四首，《戲贈》十首，雖妖冶而不耐觀，況"青衫憔悴卿憐我，紅粉飄零我憶卿"此等濫句邪！若《古意》六首則有寓意，便令人低徊欲絕。雜感之《武安席上》一首，倣《唐人本事詩》四首則有所指，故耐人探索推之。唐人玉溪[49]《無題》、冬郎[50]《香匳》莫不然也。

總之詩以言志。詩中有人方足傳其詩。梅邨以曠代逸才，遭時鼎革，不遂其高節，慙悔伊鬱，情見乎詞，而紀事論人，是非不謬，故稱詩史。後人讀其詩，哀其遇

儕之於蒙叟之麓，惜其人也！然則吾人欲作好詩，何不先學作好人乎？

46　屈原 (343 BC-278 BC)。
47　吳梅邨 (吳偉業，1609- 1671)，著有《石頭記》，後曹雪芹根據此書寫《紅樓夢》
48　趙翼 (1727-1814)，清史學家。
49　李商隱 (813-858)，唐詩人。
50　韓偓，又名冬郎 (844-923)，晚唐詩人。

SELECTED OTHER WRITINGS

Lecture On Poetry At The Chinese Society, University Of Hong Kong

Where should I begin? There is an ocean of poems, from classical to contemporary, and there are no absolute standards to judge as everyone has different tastes. In the past Master Xi'an (謝太傅) read *The Book of Poetry* and chose "The emperor should have long term goals, and should have his people in mind" (訏謨定命遠猷辰告) as the best. His brother Tze Jingsai chose "Willows swaying in the Wind" (楊柳依依), and his niece Tze Towen's favorite was "Pretty as a Breeze" (穆如清風). When we talk about poetry, it depends on the people and the situation.

Today we have many young people in the audience. I've passed my youth, but I probably understand their mentality. In poetry, the young usually favor heroic or romantic characters. But I could be a bit odd: in a heroic scene I would want the honor to go to the community. If it's romantic, I want to see how romance develops within the confines of our morals. As in *The Book of Poetry*, Wuyi (無衣) in "Feng", Changwu (常武) in "Ya", and Jianghan (江漢) , "Liuyue" (六月) , "Rouqi" (柔苣) , "Fayang" (發

揚), "Daoli" (蹈厲) *(all titles from *The Book of Poetry*) are all about the emperor and the country. The six chapters in "Changwu[even mention the emperor, which reflects the mentality of our past poets. In terms of content, nothing surpasses the woman in Xiaorong (小戎) who misses her lover so much that she feels confused, but at last decides not to be his burden. This is what the masters said about the purpose of poetry. Closer to home you can take care of your parents, and outside, you can serve your country. As they say, poetry must be about genuine feelings. Today many like to talk about flirting rather than true love. Maybe one laments as there aren't any beauties around, so he would consider courtship when he sees one. The scenario is no different from the sensational political travelogue "Zhou Qin Xing Ji" (周秦行紀), but it's been held in high regard ever since. Why? As Sima Qian (司馬遷)[1] put it: "Feng portrays true love but not lust, Ya may display grievances and criticism against the government, but it understands the moral obligations." Li Sao (離騷)[2] has both of these qualities. It may sound clichéd but people still like to talk about it, which proves that we cannot write poetry without an objective.

Young people who like modern poetry will probably love Wu Weiyi[3]. According to "Oubei Comments on Poetry" (甌北詩話)[4], he is at his best in narrative, and his poetry is touching, dainty and ravishingly beautiful. However, its quality would lack artistic appeal were it not for works like "Linjiang" "Canjun", "Yanmen Sima", "After Dong Gao School", "A walk in the Palace (殿上行)W, or "Trip to Dongloi (東萊行)". They may read like a stage without the leading cast, lavish but not touching. The

---

1 Liu Yiqing (403-444). *A New Account on the Tales of the World* 世說新語
2 Qu Yuan 屈原, (343 BC-278BC).*Warring States Period.*
3 Wu Weiye 吳偉業, alias Wu Meicun 吳梅邨 (1609-1671). Author of "The Story of the Stone" which inspired the creation of "The Red Chamber" by Cao Xueqin
4 Zhao Yi (1727-1814). Qing poet and historian

subject is fundamental, and basically loyalty or filial obligations are popular, but if every piece reads like "The Song of Chen Yuanyuan" or "The prose of Yonghe Palace," it may still be nice at the beginning and closing, but will probably be rather prosaic.

When it comes to structure, "The Flutist's Song of Green Door" could be the best. The focus was on Princess Ningde, but it first mentioned Princess Le'an, and then added Princess Rongchang. The description of their backgrounds was clear and the arrangement of their positions natural and distinctive. The entrance of Princess Cheungping at the end would not make it boring and repetitive. Indeed it began with a court concubine leading to Princess Xinyuan's residence, and ended with a dream and the curtain to dramatize the characters, and a smiling empress picking the cherries promptly echoed the beginning perfectly with all the fine details in place. In "A Poem for Jiang" (Trip to Dong Loi), the characters Song Jiuching and Jor maode entered and left the scene suddenly but this was actually arranged. Like hosting a banquet, you'd make the guests come or go at your will. If you want to learn from his poetry, pay particular attention to this.

Although Wu excelled in portraying romance with all its frills, his metaphors and hidden messages are more readable. Plain descriptions of his romantic scenes such as the four pieces on *Memories of River Qin* or the ten pieces on *Dedication* are still beautiful, but not captivating, and lyrics like "Have pity on my misfortune as I think about your loneliness."

Phrases such as (青衫憔悴卿憐我，紅粉飄零我憶卿) are clearly overused. In contrast, the implications in his , is soul-stirring and could reduce you to tears. At a Wu'an Banquet (from "Miscellaneous thoughts"), and *Imitation of Poetry from People of Tang Dynasty* (倣唐人本事詩) in four pieces have other implications which make compulsive reading. And so are Yuxi's[5] "Untitled", and Donglang's[6] "Xiang Lian".

Anyway, poetry is about making your own statement, and there must be people in the poems to convey the message. The great master Wu Weiye was unmatched in his talents, but was not accepted during his time. His honorable character was reflected in his prose. He was accurate and sharp in his narrative and arguments, and that's why they are epics. Today people are still touched by his works and his unfortunate encounters. So if we want to write good poetry, why not learn to be a good person first?

---

5   Li Shangyin, 李商隱 (813-858), alias Yuxi 玉溪. Tang poet
6   Han Wo, 韓偓 (844-923), alias Donglang, 冬郎. Tang poet

PREFACE TO "LECTURE NOTES ON POLITICAL SUMMARY OF ZHENGUAN"

When I was on duty at the South Study, I noticed some huge trunks on a shelf which were sealed and labeled. I asked the staff there and they said they were lecture notes on literature and history. Later I read *The Classic Tales of the Royal Academy* (詞林典故) which stated, "... during the second year of Qianlong, Minister Biyi (畢誼)[7] recommended that court historians prepared notes daily on philosophy and history and present them to the emperor. After deliberation among ministers and officials, it was decided that one member from the Hanlin Academy or the Attendance Court took turns to draft the lectures in the form of palace memorials, beginning with classics and history, with interpretation and explanatory notes, summaries, and remarks as appendix from the concerned official, limited to a thousand words.

Then the imperial decree arrived, which stated that the lecture folder should be written and presented daily. The emperor will

---

[7] Biyi, of Council of States. Jinshi in 57th year of Kangxi (1718)

LOYAL TO THE END

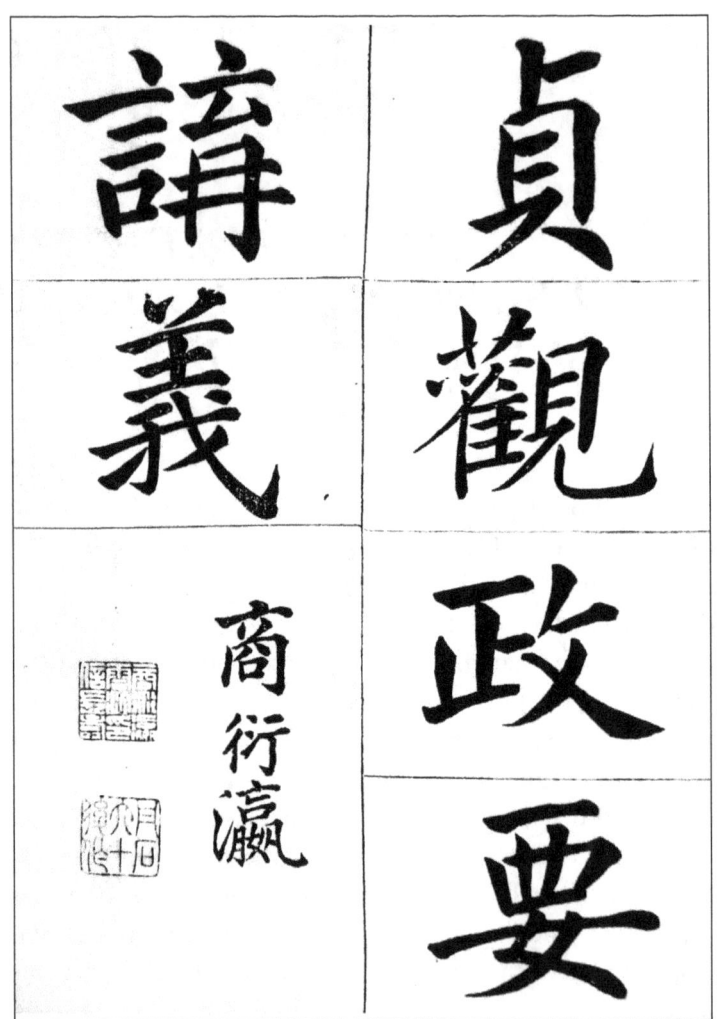

read it, and afterwards it will be kept in South Study, or members might be summoned for a discussion.

I was ordered to prepare notes the next day to be presented to the emperor, and kept in South Study afterwards. Over time, this not only helps collect views and generate resources, but the collection may also be edited into a book for reference."

After reading this, I realized this was the story behind the South Study collection.

From 1925 spring when the emperor arrived in Tianjin, I was summoned to give lectures on *The Political Summary of Zhenguan*, supplemented with notes the next day, much like the old practice. From May 1925 to August 1926, the stored lecture notes returned and packed amounted to twenty volumes. As time went on, some of these notes may have been misplaced or lost. I have edited the collection with a view to getting it printed for wider circulation, so everyone knows our emperor is so hardworking and diligent even during such difficult times. I also had on many occasions received personal advice from him which did not go on record in full due to my negligence, and I am deeply sorry for that.

蕭敬序

昔年儤直　南齋見架皮巨篋封識日久詢諸中官曰此經史講義也後閲詞林典故義乾隆二年科臣畢誼奏請令史臣日繕經史奏議進呈下王大臣議奏尋議分翰詹為一班科道為一班日輪一人具奏摺式先標經史下注義疏或節署史文下注史斷後皆附列所見日臣案云云以千言為率得　旨每日繕進書摺朕披閱後交南書房收存其或召見講論朕所降旨令本人於次日繕寫呈覽亦交南書房收存將來行之日久不特集思廣益亦可薈萃成書以資觀覽恭讀之下始悉　南齋所儲其顛未如此乙丑春從　駕莅天津奉　命進講貞觀政要講畢翌日補進講義規模署仿舊制自乙丑年五月至丙寅年八月蕆事所積存講義蒙發下分裝二十冊仍儲行在所迄今日久卷帙慮有散亡謹將稿本繕正欲付印以廣流傳使薄海內外知我　皇上學問精勤雖造次顛沛其孜孜不倦有如此者中間親承　聖訓指示者甚多惜未及一一恭紀此則微臣疏忽之愆輒引為深憾者也前南書房行走臣溫

《貞觀政要講義》自序

昔年儤直南齋，見架庋巨篋，封識日久，詢諸中官，曰：「此經史講義也。」後閱《詞林典故》載：「乾隆二年，科臣畢誼奏請，令史臣日繕經史，奏議進呈。下王大臣議奏。尋議分翰詹為一班，道為一班，日輪一人，具奏摺式。先標經史，下注義疏，或節略史文，下注史斷，後皆附列所見，曰臣按云云，以千字為率。

得旨每日繕進書摺。朕披閱後，交南書房收存，其或召見講論。朕所降旨，令本人於次日繕寫呈覽，亦交南書房收存。將來行之日久，不特集思廣益，亦可薈萃成書，以資觀覽。」

恭讀之下，始悉南齋所儲，其顛末如此。

乙丑春，從駕涖天津，奉命進講《貞觀政要》。講畢，翌日補進講義，規模略仿舊制。自乙丑年五月至丙寅年八月蕆事，所積存講義，蒙發下分裝二十冊，仍儲行在所。迄今日久，卷帙慮有散亡。謹將稿本繕正，欲付印以廣流傳，使薄海內外，知我皇上學問精勤，雖造次顛沛，其孜孜不倦，有如此者。中間親承聖訓指示者甚多，惜未及一一恭紀。此則微臣疎忽之愆，輒引為深憾者也。

前南書房行走臣溫肅敬序

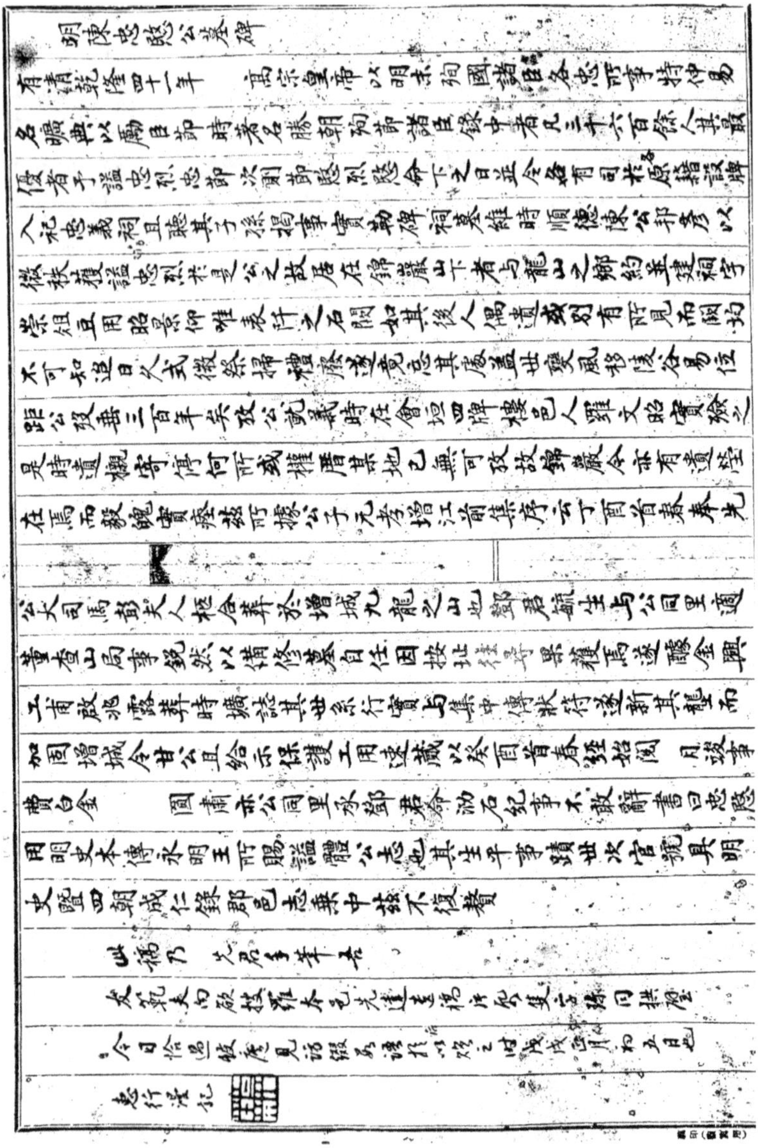

DAUGHTER AH CHIU'S OBITUARY

On September 16, 1928, I sent someone to hold a feast to pay tribute to my daughter Ah Chiu. Oh dear Chiu! how could you desert me? Your old dad is often travelling, and worried about your brothers when I pass away.

Last year I began to work on my chronology and wanted to ask you to proofread it. I was very ill this spring and I asked you to keep my will, and pledged your husband to take care of my funeral. Your uncle thought I would get well, but he died suddenly, and after a few months, I'm here mourning for you. It's because of my fate, and I'm baffled. Who is there with me? In his twilight hours, your uncle looked at you as if he had something to say, but was short of breath and his writing was illegible. Both of us relied heavily on you but you just went. How cruel you are! But that shouldn't have been what you wanted. You dismissed your illness as something minor. The night before you went, you asked when I would return to Beijing as you wanted to accompany me, and said that you would recover soon. Did you just want to console me, or did you want to return to Beijing where you were born, and keep your spirit here? Oh dear me! You were always in good health, and hadn't consulted a doctor

祭三女阿昭文

嗚呼昭乎汝竟捨吾而逝耶吾以襄年繼娶瘡執徐之歲九月望越曰辛丑阿笸遺人以酒饌殺蔬致其於亡女阿昭之靈曰

臥病晉邀啣付汝藏且託後事於汝君舅從亡在外常靡致身之後汝弟俱幼無知吾事者故去年編年體成授汝讀今春

誰耶聞汝舅彌留時願汝欲有所言而執意吾病珍而汝則遽歿越數月而聖哭汝也是豈由吾命窮所致然後顧茫茫將

汝以汝舅父付汝之重竟赧然以去亦太忍矣豈汝心哉殆以病輕忽氣喘不止命業復不成字知此心屬望於汝也

抑汝本生於吾邸然何處來測之耳殘仰一夕汝前吾何日問京欲往晉時尚謂指日可愈也豈故爲此語凶寬我懷耶

刻期往返懷身孕曾風濤跪八即從何處聞汝嘗死魂驚仍往此耶痛哉以汝氣軀之強十餘年未嘗一蹈簤門加以性情和厚形貌豐滿均無天理而其致疾

千里爲期不及四旬體汝體奕今春吾病遇暴家皆臥疾汝侍吾於病褥前萧遍嘔汝簌簌淚下傷神矣夫幾汝舅

殘汝臨歿前數日匈匆苦凶中而病益深矣是汝之死也汝以九日十二日憶去年此月此日正送汝母南旋解

纜於憎活吾望汝舟不見影乃一何奇也想汝戀母情切此時孤魂早越溟海而示夢於汝母南館時汝舅堅尼汝行吾固欲汝往爲兩全計

乎七十八歲讀四子書至十四歲毛詩戴記左傳粗能了解十五歲隨吾從入都爲吾謄貞觀政要講義稿筆意酬肯吾曹十七而

歿十八而生子使汝不聯字不嘉嫁或不至此是汝之早死吾誤之也吾誠害汝然不能無憾於汝者汝之聰明豈亦不

知此疾之沈重食少氣微形銷骨立一月餘矣終不以一字寄吾直待吾來始以實告然已不救矣欲安吾心而適增吾痛

哉吾聞古有再世而復隔世事誰能曾之況吾殘年荷遇此晤後之孤星誰憐汝者已矣

也聞汝孩姑如烟廿年直一夢即入吾目永永不忘已耳嗚呼古人云言有窮而情不可終今有酒在甑有肉在豆而汝不能食徒以有窮

昔家汝於寘漠無可有之鄉也痛哉痛哉

for over ten years. Moreover, your good nature and physique did not show any adverse signs, but there must be a reason for your illness. Last August your elder son died, and in September you took Mum home and your uncle also wanted to go with you. I of course hoped you would go. You then worked out a plan to satisfy both of us and returned here on time. Pregnant as you were, you still braved the chilling weather to travel thousands of miles in less than forty days. That hurt so much! This spring everyone in the family was taken ill and you were the only one there to take care of me. As you watched me write my will, tears rolled down your face. It must have been too much for you. Soon afterwards, your uncle passed away. You could only rest for a few days and it worsened your condition. Your death was the result of filial piety! You passed away on September 12, and it was the same day last year when you sailed southbound with Mum. I watched until the ship disappeared and returned. Curiously I thought about your love for Mum, and by this time your lonely spirit should have appeared in her dreams. My dear!

When you were three, you returned to Shunde with me. You read *The Four Books* at seven, and when you were fourteen you could understand *The Book of Poetry*, "Dai Ji", and "Zuo Zhuan" fairly well. At fifteen, you followed me to Beijing and helped me finalize the *Lecture Notes on the Political Summary of Zhenguan*. And your style closely resembled mine!

You got married at seventeen and gave birth at eighteen. Had you been illiterate and not married so early, your fate might have been different. I am the one responsible! But with your wisdom, how could you not know the seriousness of your illness? You had been eating little, weak and skinny for more than a month, but you didn't send me a word until I came, but then it was too late. You intended to comfort me but actually you hurt me so much! I heard in the past people could remain father and son in their afterlife. If your spirit is still there, you should ask to be my daughter again in your next life. But who can be sure about afterlife? I'm now old and who would pity my lonely girl? Now you are gone, and the past seems to have gone like smoke. The past twenty years are like a dream. I only hope that your son would be all right and that should make you healthier. But that was not what I saw. I only saw you curling up in pain in bed, and heard the unsettling noise from your aunt. I could never forget it. As the old saying goes, words have their limits but love knows no bounds. Now we've got food and wine here, but you can't enjoy it. I could only use my limited vocabulary to find you in the unknown wilderness. How painful, how painful!

祭三女阿昭文

維著雍執徐之歲，九月望越日辛丑。阿爸遣人以酒饌穀蔬，致奠於亡女阿昭之靈曰：嗚呼！昭乎！汝竟捨吾而逝耶！吾以衰年從亡在外，常慮致身之後，汝弟俱幼無知。吾志事者，故去年編年譜成，授汝讀。今春卧病，書遺書囑付汝藏，且託後事於汝君。舅熟意吾病痊，而汝舅遽歿。越數月而更哭汝也。是蓋由吾命窮所致，然後顧茫茫，將誰望耶？聞汝舅彌留時，顧汝欲有所言而氣喘不止，命筆復不成字，知其心屬望於汝也。以汝舅汝父付汝之重，而竟恝然以去，汝亦太忍矣！然豈汝心哉？殆以病輕忽視之耳，歿前一夕，汝詢吾何日回京，欲隨吾往。言時尚謂指日可愈也。豈故為此語以寬我懷耶！抑汝本生於京邸，從何處來，即從何處歸。將死魂靈仍注此耶？痛哉！以汝氣軀之強，十餘年未嘗一踵醫門，加以性情和厚，形貌豐滿，均無夭理，而其致疾則有由矣。客歲八月，殤汝長兒。九月送汝母南歸時，汝舅堅尼汝行，吾固欲汝往。汝為兩全計，刻期往返。懷身孕，冒風濤，踔八千里，為期不及四旬，憊汝體矣！今春吾病，適舉家皆卧疾，獨汝侍吾。見吾於病榻前書遺囑，汝簌簌淚下，傷汝神矣！未幾，汝舅歿，汝臨蓐數日，匍匐苦凶中而病益深矣。是汝之死，死於孝也！汝之死以九月十二日，憶去年此月此日，正送汝母南旋解纜於塘沽。吾望汝舟，不見帆影乃返。一何奇也！想汝戀母情切，此時孤魂早越溟海而示夢於汝母矣。痛哉！

汝生三歲，隨吾回粵，七歲讀四子書，至十四歲，毛詩戴記左傳粗能了解。十五歲隨吾復入都，為吾謄"貞觀政要講義"稿，筆意酷肖吾書。十七而嫁，十八而生子。使汝不識字，不蚤嫁，或不至此。是汝之早死，吾誤之也！吾誠害汝，然究不能無憾於汝者。以汝之聰明，豈真不知此疾之沉重？食少氣微，形銷骨立。一月餘矣，終不以一字寄吾，直待吾來始以實告，然已不救矣！是欲安吾心，而適增吾痛也。

聞古有再世而為父子者，汝靈不昧，當再託生為吾女。然隔世事，誰能言之？況吾殘年苟遺，此曙後之孤星，誰憐汝者已矣哉？往事如烟，廿年直一夢耳！所冀汝之子長成，藉此塊肉為汝增重，然豈吾所及見哉！吾所見者，只汝宛轉枕褥之狀，與汝姑攀長汝號之聲，印入吾目，永永不忘已耳。嗚呼！古人云：言有窮而情不可終。今有酒在觴，有肉在豆，而汝不能食。徒以有窮之言，索汝於冥漠無可有之鄉也。痛哉！痛哉！

LETTER FROM LI ZHANZHI

Dear In-law Buddy Pik, What a nice meal we had yesterday! I'm still full now. Thank you, thank you. My son-in-law Fan Chibun admires your calligraphy so much he has prepared four stripes, and should be most grateful if, when the mood comes, you'd splash it out, so he could keep them as his master scripts for practice.

And last year I had a fan piece (one side has already been used for landscape) begging for your work. Now spring has come and it is picturesque everywhere. Perhaps you could dig it out and compose your masterpiece for me to recite at your convenience. I'd really love it. Fingers crossed. Take care.

Respectfully,
Zhanzhi
7th (have paid for your share of birthday celebration on 9th)

黎露苑致溫肅書

檗老親家同年閣下 昨飫芳饌，今猶飽德，至謝至謝！小婿范志彬渴慕法書，謹備屏條四幅，敬乞興到為之一揮，俾得奉作楷模，至所欣幸。又去年弟有便面一幅（公面已畫山水）索公書者，邇值春暖晝長，亦乞 分神一揮，並求錄示宮扇大作，俾資諷誦，尤愜所懷。至禱至禱，泐請箸安。弟 湛枝 頓首。人日。初九日公諸祝齡已代与份矣

Reply to Li Zhanzhi's invite (Courtesy of Hok Hoi Library)

REPLY TO LI ZHANZHI'S WEDDING INVITE

復黎露苑喜柬

I opened and read your gracious letter with such a generous enclosure. Thank you for our family marriage, an honor for which I am still embarrassed[8]. Since the late Ming, our ancestors and siblings have already been connected with regional heads like Li Suiqiu[9] (黎遂球，1602-1646) through marriages for over two centuries. When it comes to social status, it may not be so much as between Hans and Manchus, yet your claim of a friendship reminiscent of Han Yu and Liu Zongyuan is something I don't really deserve. In the words of Chen Baosen, Grand Master of Luojiang (螺江太傅陳寶琛[10]) who was renowned for his pleasantries, "This marriage represents the top male and female champions in the Hall of Fame, and engraved on the plate of love." However, it must be the matchmaker somewhere who tied the knots for them long time ago. Wedding gifts in those days were mostly symbolic, like a pair of deer skin, but I guess in this

---

8   Li Zhanzhi 黎湛枝, alias Li Luyuan 黎露苑 (1870- 1928), Hanlin, Jinshi in 1903, came first in palace examination.
9   Li Suiqiu 黎遂球 (1602-1646), entrepreneur and Ming dynasty loyalist.
10 Chen Baosen 陳寶琛 (1848-1935). Qing politician, Sub Chancellor and Vice-President of Ministry of Rites.

time of turmoil, we need to observe His Majesty's austerity advice, and the tradition of giving may have to be modest. But whatever it is, I would treasure it. Moreover, you shouldn't have spent hundreds of thousands on presents, should you? But it's only ceremonial, and you can't have too much jade and silk here. Oh dear, I really don't deserve your hospitality and these luxuries. I can't accept it. No, I can't. But any way, why not?

Thank you, and do excuse my rudeness, and I'd better sign off here.

Take care, and good health. Yours respectfully,

復黎露苑喜柬

展誦華箋，更頒厚幣。既承不棄，重以婚姻。敢貢所懷，倘不河漢。昔明末吾覺斯族祖論交，嘗見重蓮鬚，迨先人及不肖弟兄兩世聯姻京兆。若論門第尚非王滿之殊。復託同年，謬附韓元之誼。以龍虎榜中之兒女注駕鴛牒上之姻緣。此螺江太傅所以有佳話之稱。實蟾窟老人定此赤繩之繫也。唯是古有納徵之禮，取物不過儷皮。今當播越之時，示儉宜遵行幄。凡茲筐篚不啻百朋，此外聘錢何須十萬？禮云禮云而已。豈宜玉帛之多！却之，却之何哉？實媿瓊瑤之報。敬拜嘉惠，藉貢蕪詞。順頌台綏統惟亮察

坂居莫問育賢坊猶有遺封嵗莟堂異代同
忠孝隼没一坏重圓玉魚葬阿山淚月傷我馬
忠孝平生痛辨無我本冬毒莹英恨生王
死士更休量

重修廣州祥雲嶺陳猛滾先生墓感生

POEM DEDICATED TO CHAN DULU ON THE RENOVATION OF HIS GRAVE IN XIANGYUN RIDGE, GUANGZHOU

Don't ask about Yu Xian Square in your past residence.
You may still find the site of the declared monument Gui Ruo Hall.
Like the dying falcon, we're in different dynasties, but our miseries are the same.
I'll take a pinch of soil to strengthen your funeral memorabilia.
The motherland before me is battered everywhere.
Loyalty and filial piety are what I treasure the most in life.
I'm just a holly in bitterness.
Dead or alive will matter no more.

重修廣州祥雲嶺陳獨漉先生墓感賦

故居莫問育賢坊，猶有遺封歸若堂。異代同悲蒼隼沒，一坏重固玉魚藏。河山滿目傷戎馬，忠孝平生竊瓣香。我本冬青曾茹恨，生王死士更休量。

溫毅夫前輩以癸亥三月拜入直南齋之命
至京得還椿樹二條衚衕故居賦此志喜

辛苦頻年類轉蓬　詔徵入直　鑒孤忠卓犖疏
議留唐殿紫鸞葉痕認漢宮薪木未傷曾子室
參苓已蓄狄公籠尋常舊物欣光復大好家居
願正同

孟秋下澣侍生朱汝珍呈稿

ZHU RUZHEN'S POEM TO WEN SU

Master Wen Su (Yifu) was summoned to South Study in March 1923. He now returns home to the two mahogany trees in the alley, and I congratulate him with this piece:

Living a hard life not your own all these years, and ordered to stand by to show loyalty.

The black eagles remain in Tang court,

While the purple swallow takes the Han palace as its home.

Zengzi's[11] house hasn't been harmed, and Di Renjie's[12] already got herbs in his basket.

Delighted to have the common old stuff revived which is what we'd all like to see.

Zhu Ruzhen[13]

gui-hai, late autumn

溫毅夫前輩以癸亥三月拜入直南齋之命至京，得還椿樹二條衚衕舊居，賦此志喜：

辛苦頻年類轉蓬，詔徵入直鑒孤忠，皁鵰疏議留唐殿，紫鷰巢痕認漢宮。薪木未傷曾子室，參苓已蓄狄公籠；尋常舊物欣光復，大好家居願正同。

11　Zengzi 曾子 (505 BC-435 BC), early disciple of Confucius, and later teacher of Mencius.
12　Di Renjie 狄仁傑 （630-700), Duke Wenhui of Liang.
13　Zhu Ruzhen 朱汝珍 (1870-1942), alias Pinsan 聘三 , Aiyuan 隘園; second in Palace examination (榜眼) in 1904.

右詩為太史朱隱園丈送先文節公奉詔入頣南之作距今二十六年矣偶檢陳篋得此喪亂之餘片紙獨在始有神護裴褫附圖末冀永其傳憶余締婚時丈實為寋修逮己卯奔喪抵里調杖履於香江承允寫先公神道碑銘宿諾未償邊悲朝露玆者手澤猶新而蓬草幾變天寒歲暮對此茫茫法然增思親懷舊之感也

戊子臘八心復謹識

RECOLLECTIONS FROM BIFU (WAN CHUNGHAN)

The poem on the right was written by uncle Zhu Aiyuan for my late father on his summons to South Study. It has now been 26 years! I found this bit of torn paper by chance when I was checking the old suitcase. It survives amid the mess as if protected by God. I have it pasted here with the hope that it will be passed on.

I remember Uncle Zhu was the matchmaker for our marriage. When I hurried home for my father's funeral, I met him in Hong Kong, and he promised to write the epitaph for his tomb tablet. However, he suddenly passed away and couldn't fulfil his pledge. Today his writing still looks fresh, but the grass at the grave has changed a few times. Amid the chill in this year end, my future looks unsettled, and I can't help reminiscing about the past and my father…

Bifu

December 8th, mu-zi year

右詩為太史朱隘園世丈送 先文節公奉 詔入直 南 (齋？) 之作，距今二十六年矣！偶檢陳篋，得此喪亂之餘片紙獨在，殆有神護！爰裱附圖末，冀永具傳。

憶余締婚時，丈實為蹇修。逮己卯奔喪抵里，謁杖履於香江。承允寫先公神道碑銘。看諾未償，遽悲朝露。茲者手澤猶新，而墓草幾變。天寒歲暮，對此茫茫，泫然僧思親懷舊之感也。

戊子臘八
必復 謹識

Council minutes (Courtesy of University Archives, HKU)

POEM TO WEN SU FROM ZHANG CIKANG (1923)

Who is this dear old friend before me? This place is famous for us Hanlins. What a good life like Wang Wendu, but you probably can't call out Meng Haoran while on duty there. In order to keep calm and remove any fury, they might resort to violence to counter integrity and determination. Now you will see the emperor while you're still alive, and I will always remember our days in Zhongli together.

So it's a farewell without wine or money, but hundreds of poems to accompany you. My works are often below those of Cao Zhi, and I need to improve anyway. Oh, I have always intended to be a hermit since I was young, but I'm afraid my works would be the best when you've left. I'm glad the virtuous and the righteous will be back to stop the evils, and you will ever be holding the gilded palace memorials.

LOYAL TO THE END

Screen at Fung Ping Shan Library, the University of Hong Kong

辦新會城閭里義塾同時在香山縣城設復廈麥
建景堂公園圖書館必甓在平縣國已復廈麥
校舍之建築必要美之支
小縣學校先生必多以支
附易小學校先生多以支
其視沈滄趣樓先生之必備建築等募捐款定
建設其學正其學正
所許多師範學校先生
建師範學校先生
凡乙丑年所建設
丁巳年自先生女公子所
手成男女公子所
助成織業十萬金募捐
助立賢資穀

亦泉此以奉記藏諸時等不募
聖人息以記諸時等不募
賢者日益興喜剝等
義心剷創學校中古
理日設經古為主學
提倡儒言論中文學院
詢為言論不可明
事旣世局不明
靈遂表彰義於是先
迫旅旋經義於是先
沈滄趣先生和偽滿是非
湯濟武先生中華不能不引退
潮美彭年文學不能不引退
沈濟伯議中學不止柳
先生張大學前己捐助
五萬餘金祭辦香港大學今
旅歸此校從旅歸辦香港大學今
用湯此校

於人仲由更得成
一天子萬南求助助藝材
霰子說作人造大學肆其華林
線諫作作人皆也川聚
於諶作作此山之也川聚
此心嶌者滋之許伊聖然選擇川桂
由作也伊聖然選擇川挂
中伊其以表退
内其以誨教不
南其必中文力表華輟
宋而詩莫力表華作
而詩力周助作起
肆志千王助
肄日周壽不
海日壽考
濱同旅揭考

賜進士出身誥授通奉大夫翰林院編修通家弟黃思永拜撰
賜進士出身誥授光祿大夫頭品頂戴賞食二品俸南書房翰林國史館總纂國史館協修現管
學部為助非
助學士
國家文

書香林古都
林院通編修家
翰檢討編通家
林之編修通弟
院通修通家溫
校家弟區大典
科計編通家弟
誥訂通修家福
庶名家家弟建
士陵弟弟恩忠
通年區決恕弟
奉侍大南金
潭學陵河港
榜讀大學北同
同士學士科
菊通士通進通
香家舉家士家
拜弟弟拜弟
祝用河用林

... AND AFTERWORD TO BIFU (1948)

In 1923, Master Wen was summoned to be on duty at South Study, I made use of a collection of poems from Su Shi[14] to send him off. He read and loved it, and said he would have it framed. Now twenty-six years later, his son Chunghan (Bifu) came under sweltering heat, showed me this painting, and requested me to write a supplement to my poem before. Wen has been gone for ten years already, and whenever I thought about my dear friend and his words, I have felt very emotional. Chunghan respectfully presented me this original piece. I was touched by his sincerity and feelings for his father, and thus I have written this to testify our years of friendship...

Sincerely,
Zhang Cikang[15] June 1948, age 76

Footnotes:
Wang Wendu 王文度 (330- 375) of Jin dynasty, son of Weng Shu 王述 (303-368), chancellor.

Meng Haoran 孟浩然 (689-740), Tang dynasty poet

Cao Zhi 曹植 (192-232), Prince of State of Cao Wei during the Three Kingdoms period, famous poet.

---

14 Su Shi 蘇軾 (1037-1101), alias Dongpo. Song dynasty writer, poet, politician.
15 Zhang Cikang 張賜康 (1873 -), Qing dynasty scholar and poet.

POEM AND POSTSCRIPT BY JIN ZHANLIN

It's been ten years since we parted, and I was deeply saddened when I looked at the painting. My memory went back to the day of farewell in Hong Kong, just before you reported for duty at South Study.

My predicament may only be understood by myself. These have been trying times, and I have failed my dear friend. My lifelong teachers and friends have become so few and far between, and I might have to wait until peace arrives to see them.

*Chunghan took leave and returned with a letter requesting me to write a supplement to the original painting "Farewell to Wen Su in Hong Kong, Autumn 1923." And I've penned these two poems to mark the occasion.

Jin Zhanlin[16]
Huo Yuan, Guangzhou
Spring 1949

---

16   Jin Zhanlin (金湛霖), alias Zi Xuan (滋軒), Qing dynasty scholar and poet.

荔公道座:昨論
還雲承、
示多荷具紉
榮蓉之周戚何不言陳光禄兄盧寧香函道
謝大約弟期待玉速必在四月不匈因誤公司船每
月開駛兩次約計是時當有船矣密切密續佈
格妹寫件項已交來一星期內阿良赴港即不帶
呈矣寧助東及姉承
道祉不一,弟囯耑
三月青

LETTER TO LAI CHI-HSI

Dear The Honorable Mr Lai,

I read your reply yesterday. Grateful that you have everything so neatly organized. What else could I say? Let me send a letter of thanks to Chan Kwonglu. The earliest time for my trip would probably be in late April as the shipping company makes two trips every month and there should be ships then. Anyway will keep you informed. Uncle Kok's script has just arrived, and Ah Leung will bring it to you once he gets to Hong Kong within a week. Sorry for this hasty response.

    Best regards,
    Su
    March 17

荔公道座　昨誦　還雲。承示各節。具紉策劃之周，感何可言！陳光祿兄處，容去函道謝。大約弟期行，至速亦在四月下旬，因該公司船每月開駛兩次。約計是時當有船矣。一切容續佈。恪叔寫件頃已交來。一星期內，阿良一赴港即可帶呈矣。率泐奉覆，附承道祺不一。

    弟 肅 頓首三月十七日。

    Council minutes (Courtesy of University Archives, HKU)

荔老四年大人閣下 月餘未修候正深
馳想滿擬此月中旬到港趁船藉抒
積忱因前日兩次玫玉伯銘託至查詢
船期竟未好覆故不成行意此公必有
別事或再告遊忘未了又今未便再玉催
詢诸
兄就近探聆此果在港頻往詢之看否
接到概玉佛竟付洪喬則请至即查
明此月下旬或下月初旬有何船赴連市迅
复一音玉为盼禱胜发
名礼不一 弟姻丽 頁十吉

LETTER TO LAI CHI-HSI

My Dear Old Lai,

It's been over a month since my last visit, and I'm always thinking about you. I thought I'd board a ship to Hong Kong in mid-month to relieve my distress, sent letters twice to Pakming the day before asking him to check shipping schedules but still haven't heard anything and so I'm stuck here. Guess this chap has something else to do or may be on his trip again. Who knows? Better not nag him this time.

Perhaps you can check it out nearby. If he's in Hong Kong, visit him and ask if he's got my mail. If it's lost, ask him to check the shipping schedules to Dalian for late this or early next month immediately. Please rush me a note, and till then,

Best regards,
Su (In bereavement)
July 11

荔老同年大人閣下：
月餘未修候，正深馳想，滿擬此月中旬到港趁船，藉抒積忱。因前日兩次致函伯銘，託其查詢船期，迄竟未得覆，故不成行。意此公必有別事或再出遊亦未可知。今未便再函催詢。請兄就近探聽。如果在港，煩往訪之，有無接到敝函。倘竟付洪喬，則請其即查明此月下旬或下月初旬有何船赴連。希迅覆一音，至為盼禱。順候台祺不一。

　　弟 期
　　蕭
　　七月十一日。
for Chan Dulu's tombstone

此稿乃先君手筆吾
友範夫囑搜揅羅本邑先達遺稿將彙集字錄同梓蟹
今日恰過彼處見話綴蕪語於此稿之时戊戌亚月初五日也
惠行漫記

MESSAGE FROM BISHEN

This manuscript is from my late father. My friend Fanfu has always wanted to collect posthumous works left by great masters of this city. Every piece and every word is treasured like rare jade. He just happened to come to my cottage for a visit, and I wrote these few words at the end of this script as a present.
 January 5, 1958
 Huixing

此稿乃 先君手筆。吾友範夫向欲搜羅本邑先達遺稿，片紙隻字，珠同拱璧。今日恰過蠖廬見訪，綴茹語於后以贈之。時戊戌正月初五日也。惠行漫記

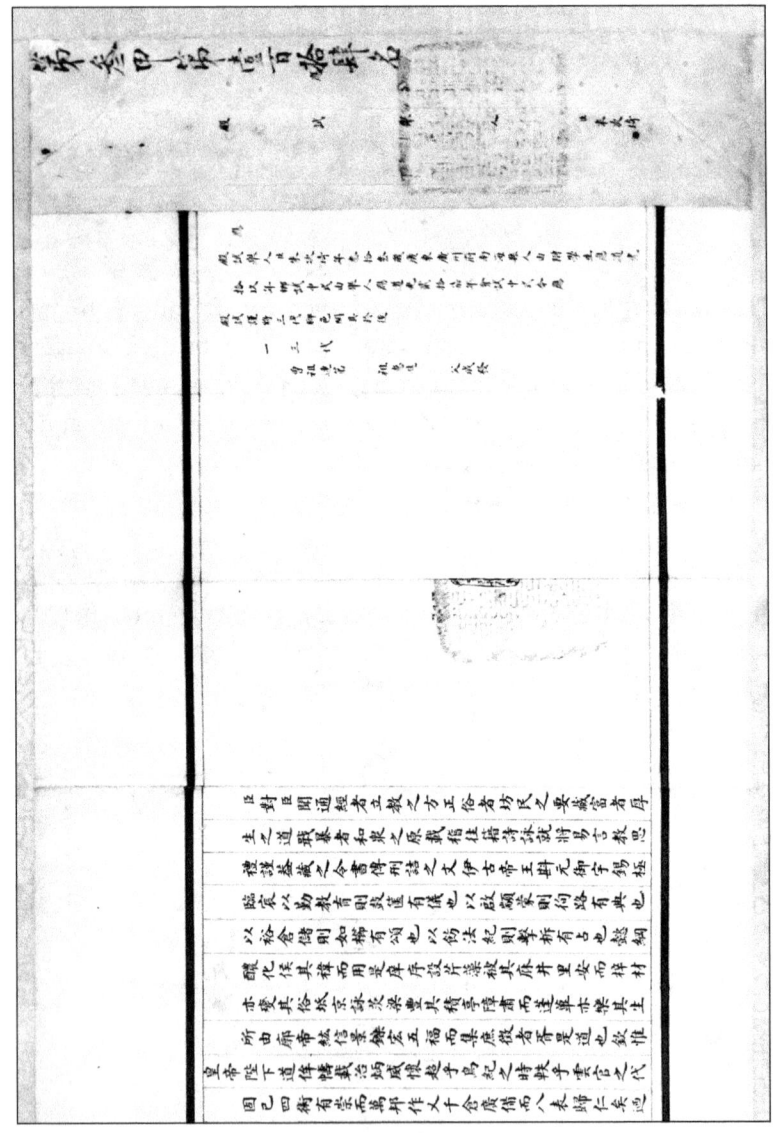

Imperial examination script of Zhu Jiujiang in 1848 (Courtesy of Richard Kan, great grandson of Kan Hungchiu, a major donor of the Confucius Hall in Hong Kong)

右朱九江先生殿試卷宣統初元清理內閣大庫積牘此卷流出都市番禺陳某淂之陳發購諸其家今攜返粵將求先生之後人歸之謹按
國朝榜運之隆向稱道光壬辰丁未二科然壬辰顯官多耳若丁未一科登揆席者三人李文忠沈文肅固赫然為中興之傑即吳江南皮相業亦一時之望餘如郭筠仙黃子壽諸公文學政術彪炳中外唯先生屈於下僚而百餘日之政績亦光照國史循吏之傳則信乎科名以人重也
此卷後注讀卷大臣姓凡八攷之當時縉紳錄蓋大學士寶興協辦大學士陳官俊尚書魏元烺侍郎季芝昌吳鍾駿朱鳳標李煌內閣學士黃琮也

戊辰嘉平月後學順德溫肅敬識

SUFFIX TO ZHU JIUJIANG'S IMPERIAL EXAMINATION SCRIPT

This Imperial Examination script (right) of Mr Zhu Jiujiang was leaked from the storeroom of the Cabinet Office during a regular cleanup of old documents in the early days of the Xuantong regime, and was bought by Chan of Punyu. I bought it back from his family after he passed away, and took it back to Guangdong in the hope of returning it to Mr Zhu's descendants.

According to records, significant achievements mostly occurred in the years of ren-chen (壬辰, 1823) and ding-wei (丁未, 1847) during the reign of Daoguang (道光). While year ren-chen had already produced quite a number of prominent officials, Ding-Wei also had three in the apex. Li Wenzhong[17] and Shen Wensu[18] were of course instrumental for our revival, and even Wu Jiang[19] and Nan Pi[20] were renowned for their ministerial careers. Others like Guo Yunxian[21] and Wang Zishou[22] were well known in literature and politics. Nevertheless, Mr Zhu was only in a humble position, but during his hundred or more days in office, performed a brilliant task that shines in our record of honorable officials. I believe it is such people who give the titles their importance.

---

17 Li Wenzhong, alias of Li Hongzhang (李鴻章 1823-1901). Qing politician.
18 Shen Wensu, alias Shen Baozhen (沈葆楨 1820-1880). Qing politician. Jinshi in 1847.
19 Wu Jiang, alias Shen Gufen (沈桂芬 1818-1880). From Wu Jiang county. Jinshi in 1847.
20 Nan Pi, alias Zhang Zhiwan (張之萬 1811-1897) From Nan Pi County. Jinshi in 1847.
21 Guo Songtao (郭嵩燾 1818-1891). Qing statesman, awarded the highest degree in Imperial Examination in 1847.
22 Wang Zishou (黃子壽 1824- 1890). Qing statesman, Jinshi in 1847.

LOYAL TO THE END

This script was read by eight examinations ministers whose names appeared in the Anthology of Gentlemen of their time. They included Bao Xing, Grand Secretary of Records; Chen Guanjun, Grand Secretary of Coordination; Wei Yuanlang, Minister; Vice Ministers Ji Zhichang, Wu Zhongjun, Zhu Fengbiao, and Li Huang; and Cabinet Secretary Wang Cong.

Respectfully,
Wen Su
December, year wu-chen (1928)

右朱九江先生殿試卷。宣統初年，清理內閣大庫積牘，此卷流出都市，番禺陳某得之。陳歿，購諸其家，今携返粵，將求先生之後人歸之。謹按國朝榜運之隆，向稱壬辰丁未二科。然壬辰顯官多耳，若丁未一科，登揆席三人，李文忠、沈文肅，固赫然為中興之傑；即吳江、南皮相業，亦一時之望；餘如郭筠仙、黃子壽諸公文學政術，彪炳中外。唯 先生屈於下僚，而百餘日之政績，亦光照國史循吏之傳，則信乎科名以人重也。此卷後注讀卷大臣姓凡八，攷之當時縉紳錄，蓋大學士寶興、協辦大學士陳官俊、尚書魏元烺、侍郎季芝昌、吳鍾駿、朱鳳標、李煌、內閣學士黃琮也。

戊辰嘉平月後學順德溫肅敬識

FRANCIS WANN

Wen Su, front row, fourth from left. (Courtesy of University Archives, HkU)

Wen Su, front row, fifth from left; Lai Chishi, sixth from left; Ou Dadian, seventh from right (Courtesy of University Archives, The University of Hong Kong (HKU)

元祐戊辰集賢林舍人招
為苕雲之游九月二日道吳
門以王維畫古帝王易于龍
圖閣待制俞獻可字昌言之
孫彥文翌日与丹徒葛藻字
季忱拾閱審定五日吳江艦
舟垂虹亭題
　襄陽米黻祕玩真蹟
　　甲戌中秋後臨米四種為
嘉孫姻世兄正　清匡溫甫

Calligraphy to in-law Lai Konin, alias LI Sun (荔孫), grandson of Hanlin Lai Chishi.
Text from Mi Fu's (米芾 1051-1107) Three Treasures Hall Inscription
(Courtesy of Alfred Lai, great grandson of Lai Chishi)

EPILOGUE

What can be read in a family letter?

Shortly before the original version of this book went to press, I unexpectedly received a few more articles which were associated with Wen Su, though they were primarily not family letters. Some were indeed poems and postscripts written by his Hanlin friends ten years after his demise as a reminder of an occasion in 1923, the year Wen Su was summoned to South Study. It was a spectacular event as Hanlins and friends lined up and offered their parting words. When Wen died in 1939 at the age of sixty-two, his son Bifu attended his funeral in Hong Kong and met Hanlin Zhu Ruzhen (朱汝珍太史) who vowed to write his epitaph. Yet Zhu died in 1942 with his word unfulfilled. Years later in 1948, when Bifu cleared his suitcase Zhu's poem mysteriously resurfaced. The paper was torn and tattered. It had been 26 years since his original poem was written, and Bifu was emotionally caught up in it. Fate had it that Bifu passed away in 1985, leaving most of Wen Su's works in the hands of Biqing, the youngest son who allegedly was looking for buyers. One of the scrolls was the painting "The Heart of Spring" (春心圖, 1917) by Qing dynasty artist Li Ru (李孺), on which up to nineteen other Hanlins and friends left their poems, postscripts, or remarks on the theme of the cuckoo, and was thought to be one of the most sought-after pieces. My friend introduced him to a potential buyer but the deal finally came unstuck. As a token gesture, he was given a few pieces which were considered of relatively little value.

One of them was that poem from Zhu, and I was instantly captured by the name. I still remember many years ago through Zhu's connection, my father was introduced to the Confucian Society and later became the Head of Confucian Primary School in Tai Hang. I looked at this torn piece of paper with the Hanlin's elegant brush strokes and my thoughts slowly went down memory lane. The passage of time has certainly left its mark, and the work has suddenly acquired its sentimental value. It wasn't quite everybody's experience to be confronted with an original piece of work from a Hanlin.

Biqing died in 2006, and the scroll was lost and has never been seen again. It has been more than a century since it first appeared.

Most of the letters in this collection were not dated. However if we read between the lines, we might find a few traces. In one of his letters to Hanlin Lai Chi-hsi, Wen signed off with the word " 期 " (qi) which indicates he was in bereavement for his wife. The year was 1929.

Some may compare his correspondence to Lord Chesterfield's letters to his son, or compare him with Sir Reginald Johnston, the diplomat who was loaned by the British Foreign Office as Pu Yi's English teacher. Others may ponder over the traditional wisdom displayed in those letters and poems. They mean different things to different people. From simply appreciation of the art of calligraphy to the more advanced research interests, they open up a window of possibilities for those who are keen to get involved in this part of history.

As a result of the research for this book, I got in touch with the descendants of some of Wen Su's contemporaries, including a few from highly influential families of their era. I am much honored to know Kenneth Fung, grandson of Fung Ping Shan; Richard Kan, great grandson of Kan Hungchiu; Alfred Lai, great grandson of the Hanlin Lai Chihsi, and Lee Chien, grandson of Hysan Lee. And recently thanks to social media, I have also linked up with Wang Liang, great grandson of Wang Guowei (王國維 1877-1927). Was it destiny that after a few generations, members of these families are reconnected?

My father would have loved this book, but sadly he did not live to see it.

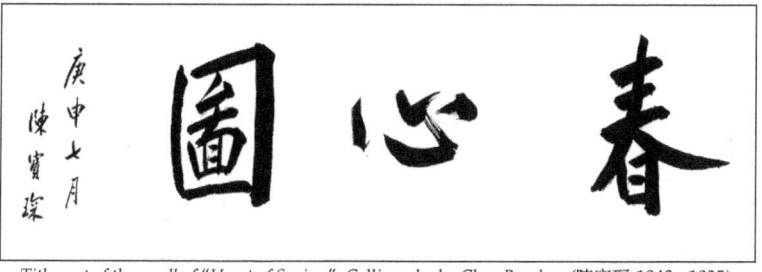

Title part of the scroll of "Heart of Spring". Calligraphy by Chen Baochen (陳寶琛 1848 - 1935), vice minister of rites

LOYAL TO THE END

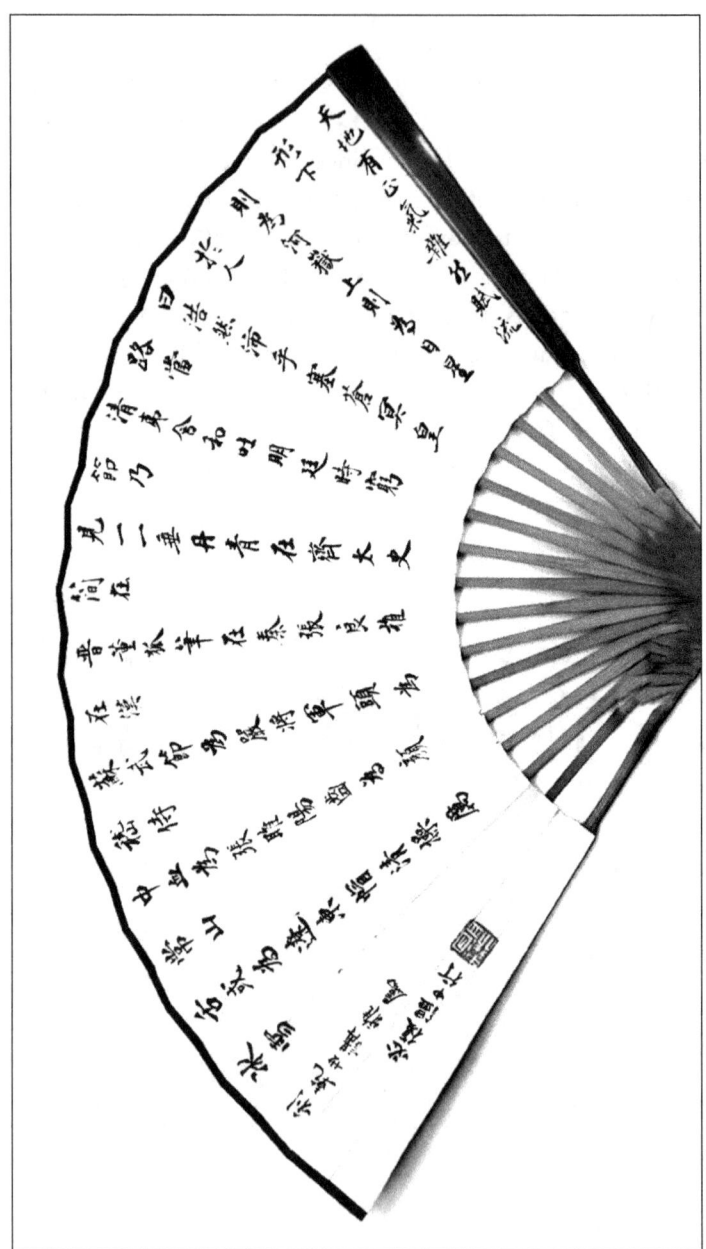

Fan piece by Bifu for Lee Chien who had studied under him. Lee is chairman of Bei Shan Tang Foundation and a governor of Lee Hysan Foundation
The Righteous Song (正氣歌) by Wen Tianxiang (文天祥), poet in South Song dynasty (文天祥 1236 - 1283)

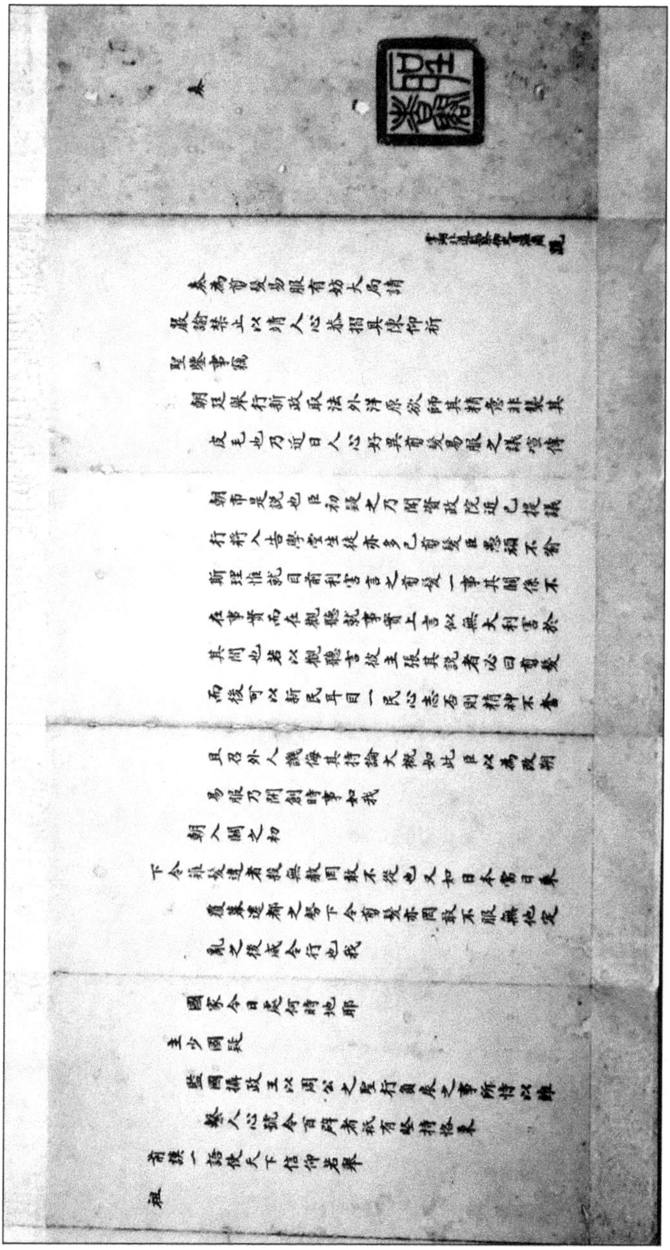

Palace memorial prepared by Wen Su

LOYAL TO THE END

AFTERWORD
DR WANG LIANG (王亮)
GREAT GRANDSON OF WANG GUOWEI (王國維),
ASSISTANT RESEARCH LIBRARIAN AND MASTERS TUTOR,
FUDAN UNIVERSITY

I have always wanted to research on the life and times of my great grandfather Wang Guowei (王國維) as well as his unpublished manuscripts and his social life among the literati. Thanks to my friends and contemporaries, my search into my family roots has often brought fresh insights. Among them is Francis Wann who has written extensively about his great uncle Wen Su (who had been in the South Study with Wang), and I am honoured to write a few words as foreword for this edition.

Wen and Wang had much in common: they were of similar age, shared similar political ideals and aspirations, were loyal to the Qing empire, and became "Qing survivors" during their prime years. Yet despite their proximity to the power corridor, they were unable to accomplish much, and finally left the political scene in despair to pursue a career in academia. The harsh reality and the sense of unfulfillment must have made them emotionally unsettled.

Regrettably over the years in my search in and out of the country, I could not find any evidence of correspondence between them. Perhaps they were not aware of it, but I believe they were both conservative and politically naive. Their unrealistic approach had finally left them to argue their case in scholarly writings.

In his lyrics "Butterfly Love Flower" (蝶戀花) as contained in "Remarks on Lyrics and the Human Existence (1909)" (人間詞話), Wang wrote "The trees fulfill their will to flourish, and show the universal love bestowed on them."(總為自家生意遂，人間愛道為渠媚)

And when he was in Tokyo for the Guichow year Poetry Gathering at the Lanting Pavilion (1913), he made reference to master calligraphers Wang Xizhi (王羲之) and Yan Zhenqing (顏真卿) : They made people wonder at their divine qualities for thousands of years, yet it was only destiny that they achieved it that day. (坐令千載嗟神妙，當日祇自全其天。—癸丑三月三日蘭亭會詩) He clearly had the foresight that his works were subject to judgements and criticisms even after his time.

Although both Wen and Wang served together at the South Study, it was Wen who actually gave lectures to Emperor Puyi on the governance of Zhenguan (貞觀之治) based on "Zhenguan Zhengyao" (Summary of Political Notes of Zhenguan 貞觀政要), and aptly deserved the title as Imperial tutor. My great grandfather, however, was posted to deal with other tasks in the palace and was indeed a far cry from the emperor's teacher.

One of the more amusing moments came from Wen Su's letter to son Bifu when he allegedly refers to Wang's calligraphy:

"The remark that calligraphy has to be unique must have come from an outsider… Works of contemporaries such as Shen Zepui (沈子培) or Wang Jing'an (ie Wang Guowei 王國維) may be considered unique, but not necessarily mastery."

Understandably Wang did not put in enough effort on calligraphy in his early years and could not master various scripts. He was nevertheless miles apart when compared against the works of Shen, Luo (Luo Zenju, 羅振玉), and Wen. However, Wang's contribution to the history and theory of calligraphy, as evidenced earlier in his Lanting Pavilion poems, clearly left his mark in the literary world today and may be considered his epic visions on calligraphy.

Wang Liang
year yisi, first month,
Shanghai

AFTERWORD
CHO-YEE TO
RESEARCH SCIENTIST & EMERITUS PROFESSOR

I am pleased to write an endorsement for this magnificient book, a collection of letters, essays and poems by an outstanding Chinese classicist and educator who lived one hundred years ago.

Wen Su (1879-1939), with outstanding academic achievements at the age of 24 (1903), after passing all the public examinations at the district and provincial levels, finally passed the imperial examination held at the palace in Beijing and attained the highest degree of Jinshi with flying colours. He was subsequently appointed to the Hanlin Academy, serving in the emperor's secretariat together with some colleagues who were a generation older. Because of his scholarly accomplishments, he later joined the then new-founded University of Hong Kong as a lecturer in Chinese classics and philosophy. He was known for his profound dedication to Chinese classical studies and art, particularly Chinese calligraphy. One of his calligraphic masterpieces consisting of ten large panels dated 1929, is on permanent exhibit at the University of Hong Kong Library.

Politically, Wen Su was truly loyal to the fallen Qing dynasty: throughout his life, he dressed traditional attire, wrote in classical style, used the lunar calendar, and celebrated the birthdays of the dethroned Qing emperor.

This volume includes Wen Su's scholarly writings, lectures, notes and his correspondence with his academic associates, friends as well as family members. Readers will, through these documents, gain knowledge and insight into his thoughts, values, life and times.

Wen Su passed away in 1939 at the age of 62, after more than two decades of teaching and promoting Chinese classical studies in Hong Kong. He and his university colleagues Hanlins Lai Chishi and Ou Dadian managed to sow the seeds for a number of younger classicists for Hong Kong. Unfortunately, under the University of Hong Kong's new leadership, the study of classical Chinese literature was deemed outdated and unimportant. This led to the abrupt termination of appointments of the Hanlin scholars in 1933. However, at that time, the scholars had already initiated their classics lectures which began in 1923 at a private venue, the Hok Hoi Library, for the public free of charge. They continued to dedicate themselves to the promotion of classical studies for the rest of their lives.

They all died several years later, before the Japanese invasion and occupation of Hong Kong in 1941.

Readers of this book will enjoy the beautiful calligraphy of Wen Su, and copies of original documents written in ink and brush. It will be one of the most significant publications of the year.

Cho-Yee To
Research Scientist & Emeritus Professor,
The University of Michigan;
Director, former Chair of Hok hoi Library Council;
Former Chair Professor of Education and Medicine,
The Chinese University of Hong Kong

AFTERWORD
DR ESTHER WOO
FUNG PING SHAN LIBRARIAN AND DIRECTOR OF
LIBRARY SERVICES
THE UNIVERSITY OF HONG KONG

Almost ninety years after the seventieth birthday of Mr Fung Ping Shan (1860-1931), I received a message from Francis asking for help to take photos of the impressive wooden screen in front of the entrance to the Fung Ping Shan Library.

The large screen was a customized gift to Mr Fung from the then Head of School of Chinese Studies, Lai Chihsi. As one of the teachers of the School, Wen Su rendered the calligraphy of the approbation about Mr Fung's contributions to the society on the screen. This delicate artifact not only reflects the indebtedness of the School to its major donor Mr Fung Ping Shan, but also signifies the long and close relationship between the School and the Library. Amazed by the efforts of Francis in researching the life of his grand uncle Wen Su, I helped seek approval from the Fung's family in granting him access to capture images of the screen for his project.

I am very pleased to see the project of Francis coming to fruition. On the eve of the ninetieth anniversary of Fung Ping Shan Library, this book is a very timely present to the Library celebrating our unwavering commitment to promote Chinese studies hand in hand with the School of Chinese and its teaching staff. We especially need more amateur historians like Francis to uncover and comb through hidden treasures to fill the gaps of the unknown past. Through the private letters and notes, the values and thoughts of Wen Su as a Hanlin in the late Qing dynasty were systematically reconstructed. This book will also provide inspiration to people who are interested in exploring or writing biography.

Dr Esther Woo
Fung Ping Shan Librarian and
Director of Library Services
The University of Hong Kong

學助國家作人之未逮其壽考必更無疆矣　先生其亦許斯
文為非貢諛乎
士出身　誥授通奉大夫　實錄館協修　國史館總纂翰林院
編修通家愚弟賴際熙頓首拜撰
士出身　誥授光祿大夫頭品頂戴　賞食三品俸　南書房翰

ACKNOWLEDGMENTS

This book would have never been produced were it not for the enormous generosity of Wu Shaolong, a prominent artist from Foshan who passed my great uncle's family letters to me, and Liang Jirong, who introduced us to each other.

During the course of writing, I received much help and advice from many others—among them, Carol Dyer of Hong Kong Women in Publishing Society for her editorial expertise, Chan Cheuk for his sharp wit, Choy Yukou for his unwavering encouragement, Wong Yeemei for proofreading, and above all, Ho Yauwei for his masterly brushstrokes which grace the cover of this book.

I am also indebted to Dr Esther Woo, Fung Ping Shan Librarian, the University of Hong Kong; Dr Cheung Ngaiyee of Bei Shan Tang Foundation, Garfield Lam of University Archives, HKU; Lee Chien of Lee Hysan Foundation, Prof Li Lin of East China Normal University, China; Prof Lee Hokming, Emeritus professor at Hong Kong Metropolitan University, HK; Prof Hung Siuping, Emeritus professor at Shue Yan University, HK; Kenneth Fung, grandson of Fung Ping Shan; Alfred Lai, great grandson of Hanlin Lai Chishi; Wen Shanglian, grandson of Wen Su; Lee Hingyan, former Chinese correspondence manager, Heng

LOYAL TO THE END

Seng Bank, HK; Lord Wilson of Tillyorn KT GCMG FRSE, past governor of Hong Kong; and Roy Allen, teacher and longtime friend. All of them offered their invaluable insight and assistance at various stages of production. Any shortcomings in this book are entirely my responsibility.

Last but not least, I am much honoured to have the afterwords by Prof Choyee To, past president and former chairman of Hok Hoi Library, research scientist & Emeritus professor of education at University of Michigan, USA; and Dr Wang Liang, Assistant Research Librarian and Masters Tutor at Fudan University, China, and great grandson of Wang Guowei. Besides, I should also mention Shirley, the accidental photographer who took the last snapshots of the couplet; John, who started off this literary journey of inquiry with me some three years ago; and Sabina, who inspired me to write.

BIBLIOGRAPHY

KWOK Waiting. "An Inquiry of Mr Wan Chunghan's Posthumous Manuscripts"(溫中行先生生平與詩詞遺稿初探), 2012. *An Anthology of Literary works in Longjiang, Longjiangzhen People's Government.*

"Calligraphy from Hanlin Masters" (翰墨流芳). 2003. Hok Hoi Library.

Earle. H.G. "An Imperial Policy in Education with special reference to the University of Hong Kong". 1927. Hong Kong: Norona.

Hucker, Charles. "A Dictionary of official titles in Imperial China". 1985. Southern Materials Centre.

Lai, T.C. "A Scholar in Imperial China—A Biography of Lai Chishi, 1970. Kelly & Walsh.

Li, Lin. "The Last Hanlins—A Study of Jinshis and Jinshi Academy in Late Qing. 2014". Tsin Hua Journal of Chinese Studies.

Li, Shuxian. "My husband Pu Yi, the Last Emperor of China." 2008. China Tourism Press.

Records of Cultural Inheritance in Hong Kong (香海傳薪錄). 2008. Chinese Cultural and Historical books Publishing Ltd.

Pu Jie, Pu Yi. "From Emperor to Citizen". 1961. Xinhua Bookstore.

Wen, Su. *Anthology of Collected Works* (温文節公集), 2001. Hok Hoi Library.

Wen, Su. *Lecture notes on Political Summary of Zhenguan*. 1936.

Wen, Su. *Collected works of couplets and poetry*. 2008. Chung Wanman(Ed)

Zhu Ruzhen. *A Collection of Essays*. 1990. Guangling Rare Books Blockprinting Ltd.

About the Author

Francis Wann (雲中燕) is a producer, photographer, editor and teacher. He has a PhD in Semiotics and is the author of *THE OTHER WEN SU* (温肅別傳), and the translator/editor of the poetry anthology LET IT BE by Lujah. He is an occasional features writer for Leica International. *franciswann8@gmail.com*

www.ingramcontent.com/pod-product-compliance
Lightning Source LLC
LaVergne TN
LVHW012014060526
838201LV00061B/4307